I0510649

Equipped for Project

Entrepreneurship

Dealing with change in disruptive times

by Barbro Moen Ternsten

Copyright 2017 by Barbro Moen Ternsten, Notodden, Norway.

All rights reserved.

Dedication

This is for you, Mom.

Thank you for always being there for me. Thank you for letting me become who I have become, and for supporting me through all my decisions in life. Thank you for holding my back in difficult times, and for always being there to talk through the amusing and exciting moments and the more complicated situations in my life. Thank you for having an open mind, which has affected the way I look at the world, and the people I have encountered on my journey through life. Thank you for learning me that whatever comes to you, you will have to deal with, one way or the other. And, for being one of the strongest women I know. Thanks for not stopping me when I was a little girl and wrote copies of books into my notebook by hand. I guess it all makes sense now.

Finally, Eivind Jørgensen and Elisabeth Langekjend, thank you for valuable feedback and input on the book. You people are great!

Table of Contents

Table of Figures

Introduction

Are you prepared to take the next leap in your career? I mean taking the lead in changing the way your company provide products, services or other results to your customers. Because, we know for sure, that the way your company provide these products, services or results to your customers today, will change. Either the product or service itself will change, or the way you provide these products or services will change, or (I predict), it is highly likely that both previously mentioned scenarios will happen.

In order to cope with this ever-changing business environment, it will become more and more demanding for people employed in technical service organizations to deal with change. Especially for those people working closely with change management, business innovation, and the means to implement them: the projects.

In this book, I will draw on literature within the fields of innovation, knowledge work, systems thinking, change management, project management, portfolio management, and at the same time, I will contribute to these topics with real-life experiences as a line manager, project manager and portfolio manager. I am sharing these experiences because I strongly believe that while theory is a good foundation to build upon, actual experience, should never be under-estimated, nor neglected.

Personal Remarks

Let me start by saying that I am not a professional author, or writer, for that matter. I am a professional businessperson with extensive experience in the fields of information technology, project management, portfolio management, change management and leadership. For about 10 years, I have had this emergent desire to write a book, circling the fields I have been working in throughout 20 years in different companies in Norway.

I consider myself a knowledge worker, and therefore, this book will talk a lot about the typical context for such workers, and the challenges faced in knowledge-intensive companies. I have worked as a consultant and as an employee in many different manager positions, and my current position is as Head of Product Development for a telecom company in Norway. I also hold the role as Project Portfolio Manager.

Wearing these hats, I try to think of myself as a technology broker. Working with development projects and incremental innovations requires me to step out of my comfort zone quite often, and by doing this, I also learn and acquire knowledge from many other disciplines across the company, and outside of the company. I would actually argue that writing this book is a result of technology brokering. You might not have heard of technology brokering before. Well, then I guess my advice would be to continue reading this book.

During my 20+ years in different roles within several organizations, I have invested a lot of time in IT development projects both in Norway and internationally, but also in process and product development projects across different sectors. I have gained experience in different cultures, different methods and methodologies, different worldviews, and I have collaborated with people across all functional areas within a typical organization. I thrive in organizational environments that enforce autonomy within teams, the right level of structure, and that provide workers with sufficient governance to secure the evaluation, acceptance and implementation of change initiatives in the best way possible. As a portfolio manager, off course, my DNA is all about doing the right things, and secondly, doing the things right.

Change and Innovation

Introduction

"Discovery is seeing what everybody else has seen, but thinking what nobody else has thought (Albert Szent-Györgyi)."

The following topics are covered in this chapter:

- Disruptive organizations
- Innovation
- Technical Service Organizations
- What is knowledge?
- Managing Knowledge Workers and Knowledge Work
- Project Entrepreneurship

Disruptive organizations and innovation

You can divide your organization's activities into two main categories: *business as usual* and *change*. Business as usual involve repetitive, ongoing activities, such as manufacturing, service, and production, whereas change (mainly implemented through projects) involve unique, one-time initiatives, such as launching new products, new organizations, or new ventures, improving existing products, and investing in the company's infrastructure.

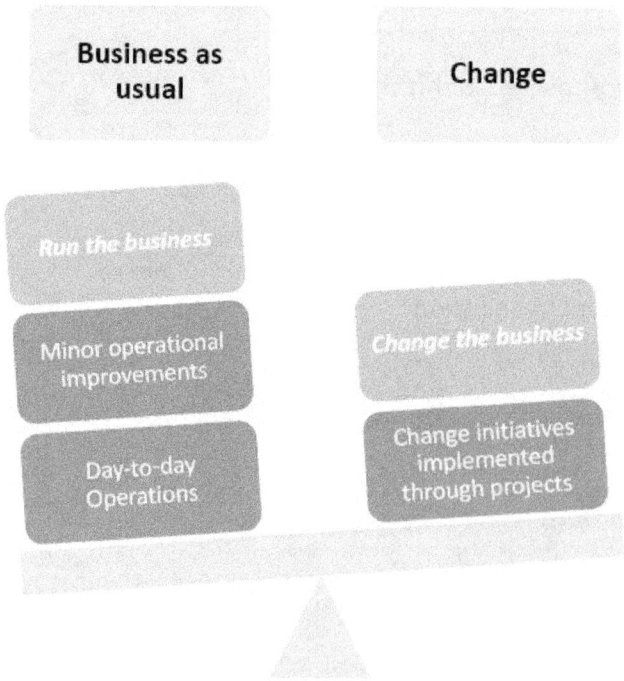

Figure 1. An organization's main activities: Business as Usual and Change.

Projects drive business innovation and change. In fact, the only way organizations can change, implement a strategy, innovate, or gain competitive advantage is through projects. Furthermore, if you think about it, every business as usual process began as a project that put things into motion (Shenhar & Dvir, 2007).

In earlier years, the dominant approach to addressing organizational change was to treat it as a one-time event. Often described as the organization normally existing in a stable, "frozen" state, then the status quo was "melted" by a change event and then "refrozen" into a new norm (Pat Durbin & Terry Doerscher, 2010). Because change events were considered relatively rare and unique occurrences, there was little reason to have standard policies and processes to manage them. Today, we view change as a constant reality for modern organizations; we are always in a state of change. Portfolio management processes provide a disciplined approach to anticipate and manage both revolutionary and evolutionary changes in a consistent, repeatable, and transparent way. Let us start by looking into the theory of innovation.

Theory of Innovation

My favourite definition of innovation is, *seeing what everybody else has seen, but thinking what nobody else has thought.* Some might think of this as a simplification of innovation, but in my experience as a knowledge worker, this is where it usually starts. Back in the industrial age, innovation was often related to inventions of concrete products, such as the washing machine or the microwave oven. Nowadays, more and more organizations deliver services to their customers, and inventions would be the wrong word to use to describe the continuous improvements and launches of new services within these industries. Actually, in most cases, it is the recombination of existing technologies in some markets, implemented in other markets, which constitutes a fair amount of today's innovations. *Innovation is about connecting, not inventing.*

Then there is the distinction between incremental innovation and radical innovation. While incremental innovation can be described as a series of small improvements to existing product, service, process, organization or method whose performance has been significantly enhanced or upgraded, a radical (or disruptive) innovation is one that has a significant impact on a market and on the economic activity of firms in that market. I often think of radical innovations as a change that *eliminates some core competences of the organization.*

There is a huge amount of literature available on different types of innovations; being architectonical innovation, global and local innovation, product and process innovation, technical innovation and administrative innovation. For now, let us only wrap our heads around incremental and radical innovation, keeping in mind that the latter is rarer.

Technical Service Organizations

The reason for my focus on technical service organizations is simply the fact that they are increasing in number, and it happens to be a category, which I am very familiar with. Secondly, it might prove to be even bigger challenges in dealing with change within these organizations. Let me get back to that.

The technology revolution that began in the 1980s set the stage for today's constant change and compressed time to market, which led to rapid growth in business sectors that use knowledge workers to provide technology-based services (Pat Durbin & Terry Doerscher, 2010).

Technical service organizations can come in many flavours and forms – they can be companies providing specific services directly to the end customer, or they could be departments or business units within a larger organization. Technical service organization rely on knowledge workers. The typical competence held by knowledge workers span over areas such as engineering services, product development, research and development, IT services, to name a few. The basis of the operation they perform is the knowledge of the individuals themselves. In opposition to industrial workers, where the basis of the operation they perform is the structure of activities. Where industry work represent routine work, knowledge work represent non-routine work.

So what are the typical characteristics of technical service organizations (TSOs)? Typically, TSOs share the following characteristics (Pat Durbin & Terry Doerscher, 2010):

- They serve multiple internal and/or external customers with virtually unlimited needs, resulting in an opportunity-rich environment.
- They have responsibilities to simultaneously facilitate change and manage ongoing operations (business as usual).

- They deal with a high volume of inbound work of different types, ranging from strategic projects to level-of-effort support requests.

- Their primary mechanism of producing deliverables is through the talents of a limited number of skilled, specialized, professional knowledge workers.

- A significant portion of this staff multi-tasks across a range of different assignments and responsibilities.

- Resources are arranged in a matrix organizational structure, with various groups dependent on one another to achieve useful results.

- Staff members function in a dynamic business environment where strategies and priorities are constantly being adjusted in response to the ever-increasing pace of business, new opportunities, and rapidly evolving technology.

- Many times projects cannot be fully planned and staffed in advance due to the iterative nature of the work or use of new technology.

- The elusive nature of knowledge-based work requires different measurement and control methods compared to creating tangible deliverables from physical materials.

Managing Knowledge Workers

Managing knowledge work and knowledge workers is arguably the single most important challenge being faced by all kinds of organizations. This is because innovation is so central to knowledge work – many of the unique skills and experiences of knowledge workers would be largely wasted if they were not provided with the opportunity to put these skills to work in order to do things differently and to innovate. Innovation also entails the application of knowledge to new tasks and situations in order to develop products, processes and services, and is a prime site for knowledge work (Newell et al, 2009, p. 187). In short, in a service economy, innovation is fundamentally about managing knowledge and knowledge work (Coombs, 2003; Miles, 2003).

We will have to dive into the theory of knowledge as well. This will not be a deep dive, but I will refer to the most important areas of knowledge and knowledge management as I see it. The philosophy of what knowledge is has been a debate since the classical Greek period. We will start by referring to the *"epistemology of possession"* and the *"epistemology of practice"* (Cook and Brown, 1999). While the epistemology of *possession* treats knowledge as something people have, the epistemology of *practice* treats knowledge as something people do. Hence, we can see that knowledge – or claims to knowledge – are social as well as individual and depend heavily on the organizational and cultural context in which such claims are made (Newell et al, 2009). To put it short, I think we can conclude that a combination of these two philosophies is a reality when we continue to talk and discuss knowledge and knowledge workers. In the book, *Managing Knowledge Work and Innovation* (Newell et al, 2009) they define knowledge as *"the ability to discriminate within and across contexts"*. They also stress that there are three dimensions of knowledge work: *enabling contexts, purposes* and *processes*. Furthermore, a completely new language has arisen around concerns that it is knowledge, and no other resources such as labour or capital, that is the main source of competitive advantage across sectors (Newell et al, 2009, p. 21). In 1969, Drucker emphasized that knowledge had become the crucial resource of the economy. Daniel Bell, in 1973, also described the potential for the development of a post-industrial society dominated by knowledge workers operating in knowledge-intensive firms. This would be a society organized around knowledge for the purpose of economic development, social control and institutional innovation and change (Newell et al, 2009, p. 22).

There is one real life example, which comes to my mind when discussing the topic of knowledge workers and innovation. Google. It has grown from a two-man start-up (in 1998) to an organization with nearly 57.000 employees (Q2 2015) in more than 40 different countries. Having visited the Google headquarters in Mountain View, California myself, I have to admit that this company has truly done something different from most others. Google has devoted an enormous intellectual firepower to discover, refine, and implement leadership practices that optimize human performance in the workplace. In their very early days, the founders Larry Page and Sergey Brin, set their sight on making Google a truly great place to work. Determined to attract and retain great talent, they went in search of organizations that had proven histories of caring for people, driving extraordinary innovation, and building truly remarkable brands. They identified the SAS Institute as being the one company worth emulating. After the founders met personally with SAS executives, they validated their understanding that people truly thrive in their jobs – and remain loyal to them – when they feel fully supported and authentically valued. Few, if any businesses ever, have been built with employee happiness as its cornerstone. They relied on business guru Peter Drucker and his understanding of how to manage the breed of "knowledge workers". Drucker stated that knowledge workers believe they are paid to be effective, not to work 9 to 5, and that smart businesses will *"strip away everything that gets in their knowledge workers' way."*

What better example of a business competing in the service economy, relying on knowledge work and continuous innovation is there? In fact, getting the most out of knowledge workers has been high on the agenda ever since the foundation of the company. They even have established 10 golden rules for knowledge workers:

1. **Hire by committee** – if you hire great people and involve them intensively in the hiring process, you'll get more great people. *"That means we're harnessing energy rather than coaxing it out of people"*.

2. **Cater to their every need** – *"strip away everything that gets in their way"*. Let's face it: programmers want to program, they don't want to do their laundry. So we make it easy for them to do both.

3. **Pack them in** – every project in Google is a team project, and teams have to communicate. Virtually everyone at Google shares an office.

4. **Make coordination easy** - In addition to physical proximity, each Googler e-mails a snippet once a week to his work group describing what he has done in the last week.

5. **Eat your own dog food** - Google workers use the company's tools intensively. For example, one of the reasons for Gmail's success is that it was beta-tested within the company for many months.

6. **Encourage creativity** - Google engineers can spend up to 20 percent of their time on a project of their choice. There is, of course, an approval process and some oversight, but we want to allow creative people to be creative.

7. **Strive to reach consensus** - at Google, the role of the manager is that of an aggregator of viewpoints, not the dictator of decisions. Building a consensus sometimes takes longer, but always produces a more committed team and better decisions.

8. **Don't be evil** - we foster to create an atmosphere of tolerance and respect, not a company full of yes men (particularly in the ranks of management).

9. **Data drive decisions** - at Google, almost every decision is based on quantitative analysis.

10. **Communicate effectively** - every Friday we have an all-hands assembly with announcements, introductions and questions and answers.

A final note taken from Google's 10 golden rules for knowledge workers:

"We have focused on managing creativity and innovation, but that's not the only thing that matters at Google. We also have to manage day-to-day operations, and it's not an easy task. We are building technology infrastructure that is dramatically larger, more complex and more demanding than anything that has been built in history. Those who plan, implement and maintain these systems, which are growing to meet a constantly rising set of demands, have to have strong incentives, too. At Google, operations are not just an afterthought: they are critical to the company's success, and we want to have just as much effort and creativity in this domain as in new product development."

Having worked in knowledge-intensive firms about 20 years myself, I still have not seen a fully workable approach to manage knowledge workers in terms of enabling contexts, purposes and processes, but rather partly implemented in certain pockets within the organization. However, what I have seen is that there are managers out there who fully understands how dependent the firm is on these knowledge workers and the specialist skills they hold. Other managers, on the other hand, have not yet realized that knowledge workers are the organization's primary means of production (unlike Google). It is undoubtedly hard for the traditional manager to realize that knowledge work cannot easily be captured, filed and standardized, and therefore it is difficult for such managers to give knowledge workers the needed autonomy in performing their work and to make their own decisions.

All of this poses new challenges for management in knowledge-intensive organizations (Newell et al, 2009, p. 26):

- Develop *enabling contexts* – including organizational cultures, structures, and opportunities for collaborative forms of work and coordination, reward and recognition systems and career opportunities.

- Understand *knowledge processes* – that is the process and practices through which knowledge is shared, integrated, translated and transformed.

- Deploy knowledge for specific *purposes* – that is to accomplish specific tasks as set by particular interest groups.

- Align *contexts, knowledge processes and purpose* in the management of knowledge work.

Dealing with innovation in Technical Service Organizations

A major purpose for knowledge workers is to drive innovation. They might not be conscious about driving innovation, but indeed, they are. Imagine the sum of small to medium product development projects in any technical service organization. It is easy to argue that these small improvements and developments will, as years add up, lead to incremental innovation, and possibly radical innovation as well. Taking into the picture that innovation is more than often complex, uncertain, torturous, and a highly political activity, you set the perfect stage for a knowledge worker. They operate in this environment, day in and day out. No wonder we are searching for better ways to handle innovation processes. The only thing that is certain is that a single "best practice" approach to managing knowledge work is highly problematic.

Some scholars even argue that "material products" are themselves only material embodiments of the services they deliver (Dankbaar, 2003, p. 79). It can even be difficult to tell whether we are actually buying a service or a product. The implications of the rise in services for managing knowledge work are extensive. With service innovation, relevant knowledge is nearly always distributed across a whole range of stakeholders, including, on a much greater basis than before, the customer (Dodgson et al, 2005). Knowledge workers also need significant autonomy so that they can deal flexibly with customers that are more knowledgeable and actively match services to requirements. Indeed, the links between knowledge and innovation, and the virtue of knowledge management for improving innovations, are rarely questioned in the literature (Newell et al, 2009, p. 187).

Taking another look at the *"epistemology of possession"* and the *"epistemology of practice"*, for example from the *"knowledge as a possession"* point of view, there is no particular reason, why innovation should follow from increased quantities of knowledge – indeed information overload might quite conceivably reduce innovative capability. Equally, from a *"knowledge as a practice"* perspective, knowledge required to develop and implement innovation is often widely distributed amongst individuals, groups, organizations, even nations and cultures. Innovations does not automatically result. These dynamics needs to be considered carefully in understanding whether and how knowledge can be managed to achieve innovation (Newell et al, 2009, p. 188).

Whilst most work in innovation has focused on the design and development of products, the growing importance of services has made process innovation as, if not more, important. Innovations in services seems to have distinctive characteristics that pose particular challenges for managing knowledge work – challenges that are summarized by Newell et al (2009) in the figure below. It is worth remembering that product and process innovations do pose potentially different problems for managing knowledge. Knowledge creation in product innovation, for example, tends to converge around the product itself. This means that the product – and associated physical artefacts such as blueprints and prototypes – can serve as tangible "boundary objects" in bringing together relevant knowledge (Whyte et al, 2008).

Characteristics	Description	Challenges for managing knowledge work
Intangible	The value of the knowledge cannot easily be demonstrated in advance of the service actually being used.	• Protecting intellectual property, patenting against piracy • Persuading people to use the service in advance of proof of effectiveness
Interactive	New and more interactive models of development and delivery require knowledge distributed across a wider range of stakeholders (including customers and end users). Production of knowledge simultaneous with consumption.	• Knowing what knowledge people have. • Getting relevant knowledge workers involved in the innovation process. • Can involve service provider innovating at the clients' premises (e.g. consultancy services).
Information intensive	Variety of information and models of information delivery involved.	• Using forms of information and modes of information delivery that are seen as accessible, of interest and legitimate by varied service users.
Heterogeneous	Different opinions as to the value of the information and what constitutes a good service.	• Understanding and accommodating stakeholder interests and viewpoints. • Can generate tensions between standardization and customization.
Interdependent	Users of services (e.g. professionals) more powerful in relation to them because they are intangible and difficult to legitimate in advance.	• Enrolling powerful professional users and/or service regulators. • Developing professional standards and networks to legitimate new knowledge.

Figure 2. Service Innovations and challenges for managing knowledge work.

In contrast, knowledge produced through process innovation is largely intangible, tacit and context-dependent. It will typically include knowledge related to changes in work practices, changes in roles and responsibilities, and changes in attitudes and cultural values. This process knowledge is difficult to codify, at least in ways that could be easily understood when transferred to new contexts. Social and behavioural processes are therefore likely to be as, if not more, important to managing knowledge for process innovation than practices aimed at codification. For example, Hansen et al (1999) found that *"personalization strategies*" (the development of intensive personal relationship and social networks) were more effective than codification strategies where the knowledge to be transferred was largely tacit in nature. This broad difference between product and process innovation again highlights the need to be sensitive to the purpose of the innovation when designing strategies and approaches to managing knowledge.

Taking change seriously

Change is everywhere, it is entering our organizations in an impressive speed, and we know for sure that the pace will continue to increase. So, what does this mean for you and me, as typical knowledge workers? Hang on to that question just a bit, while we look at some interesting numbers.

PMI estimated that there were 16.5 million Project Managers in the world per October 2011. Between 2010 and 2020, 15.7 million new project management roles will be created globally, and the project management industry is slated to grow by $6.61 trillion. This means that we are probably talking about 30 million project managers out there, working every day to implement changes to their organizations.

Knowledge-intensive firms describes those firms where the majority or even the entire workforce consists of knowledge workers. Alvesson (2004) distinguishes between two major types of knowledge-intensive firms; R&D companies and professional service firms. Professional service firms deal largely with intangibles and those employed often deal directly with clients, while R&D companies typically produce tangible products and contact between employees and the customer are less direct.

Project-intensive industries describe those in which occupational employment has a high level of project-oriented work. In general, these industries are manufacturing, business services, finance & insurance, oil & gas, information services, construction, and utilities.

With this in mind, has the management team in your organization realized how much of the daily activities and efforts in your organization which are connected to knowledge work and project-oriented work? I am sure that most management teams today have not yet fully realized the ratio between *Change* and *Business as Usual* (BAU). That is partly the reason for writing this book.

With this in mind, here are a few statements for taking change seriously:

- No organization can survive today without successful projects and the minds of Project Entrepreneurs.

- Project Entrepreneurs will play a crucial role in organizational change and innovation.

- Management teams need mentoring and highly skilled knowledge workers to help them understand this landscape, and to implement necessary and sufficient governance models and portfolio management processes to deal with change.

Now, let us get back to that question, what does this mean for you and me? How are we supposed to inform the management team that we need to take this seriously?

I remember the first months of my current job in a Norwegian Telecom company. Hired as an IT manager, and having background from Project Management and especially Project Portfolio Management, I was asked by my manager to make a report on how we currently were handling projects. The report ended up being devastating. Out of 19 projects executed in 2013, five of them had a written project charter, none of them had an approved budget, and ten of them had a project manager. The total spending was about 66 million NOK. I was invited to a management team meeting the following week to present my findings. I showed them these exact numbers and facts, and bluntly asked them one question – who feels comfortable that this is the best way to invest our money in IT development (and innovation)?

Project Entrepreneurship

I participated in an innovation program in the Norwegian Business School a few years back. The lecturer used this definition of entrepreneurship. *The pursuit of opportunity beyond the resources you currently control.* Being an entrepreneur is all about visioning the future into the present. More importantly - not taking no for an answer.

Aaron J. Shenhar, a leading scholar in project management, and a Professor of Management at the Stevens Institute of Technology, has personally given me new inspiration to think differently as a project manager. I attended his training class in Oslo in 2015, called SPL Foundation, Strategic Project Leader. In his book - *Reinventing Project*

Management – he talks about the challenges of addressing the complex problems of today's projects. He claims that most project problems are not technical but managerial. When projects fail, usually management failed to put the right system in place so that errors can be detected in due time. The critical questions are these:

- *Can we help project teams make the right assessment before presenting their project proposals to top management?*
- *Can we show executives how to ask the right questions and foresee danger before they make a commitment to a project and before it is too late?*

In his book, Shenhar offers a new framework in which the project management style can be tailored to the circumstances, environment, and task. The traditional model – derived from the two fundamental drivers; *The triple constraint* and *One size fits all*, is according to Shenhar, only viable for a small group of projects today. Most modern projects are uncertain, complex, and changing, and they are strongly affected by the dynamics of the environment, technology and markets (Shenhar & Dvir, 2007).

To solve this dilemma, Shenhar proposes to use a more adaptive approach to project management, and he presents the *diamond approach*, covering four dimensions: novelty, technology, complexity and pace. I will briefly explain the four dimensions here.

Dimension	Explanation	Types (scale)
Novelty	This represents the uncertainty of the project's goal, the uncertainty on the market, or both. It measures how new the project's product or service is to the customers, users or to the market in general and thus how clear and well defined the initial product requirements are.	Derivative, Platform, New to the market, New to the world
Technology	This represents the project's level of technological uncertainty. It is determined by how much new technology is required.	Low-tech, Medium-tech, High-tech, Super-high-tech
Complexity	This measures the complexity of the product or service, the task, and the project organization.	Component, Assembly, System, Array
Pace	This represents the urgency of the project – namely, how much time there is to complete the job.	Regular, Fast/competitive, Time-critical, Blitz

Now, let me explain the idea behind *Project Entrepreneurship*. For all our professional lives, we have made the distinction between project owner (sponsor) and project manager. The first being responsible for the project outcome and its impact on the business, and the last being responsible for the project output (and primarily being focused on meeting timelines, budgets and deliver according to scope). Shenhar has a different way of looking at this. He believes that project managers should take on more responsibility, and that project and product success should not be separated. In my own words, he would like us to take on the role of the *project entrepreneur*. Now, it has to be said that not all organization are willing to let the project manager take on the role as the project entrepreneur, but then again, have we ever offered this possibility to our management team? Have we ever really tried to re-invent the way we manage projects? Have we not neglected the obvious fact that for those of us who have the DNA of a project entrepreneur, we would be able to succeed better with our projects if we were given the responsibility for the product success as well? I know that many project managers out there do have the DNA of a project entrepreneur, and I am so convinced that one of the most important ingredients to succeed with innovation in the future (and project and product success altogether) is to embrace these project entrepreneurs. Let them get the autonomy needed to build

project success AND product success.

The relevance of Systems Thinking

Introduction

"Simplicity is rarely effective in the face of complexity, change and diversity."

The following topics are covered in this chapter:

- Systems Thinking
- Reductionism vs Holism
- Organizational cybernetics
- Viable system model (VSM)
- Creativity
- Systems thinking and common metaphors

What is Systems Thinking?

Senge (1990) defines Systems Thinking as *a discipline for seeing the "structures" that underlie complex situations, and for discerning high from low leverage change*. Ultimately, it simplifies life by helping us to see the deeper patterns lying beneath the events and the details. I will say yes to anything that would simplify my life. For sure. Before we can include system thinking into our context of changes in our organizations, I will take you through a short history of systems thinking and the evolvement into today's prevailing theories.

A system could be many things, and they come in different types, some examples taken from Michael C. Jackson's book called Systems Thinking – Creative Holism for managers (2003) – are:

- physical, such as river systems

- biological, such as living organisms

- designed, such as automobiles

- abstract, such as philosophical systems

- social, such as families

- human activity, such as systems to ensure the quality of products

The traditional method for studying such systems is known as reductionism. Reductionism sees the parts as paramount and seeks to identify the parts, understand the parts and work up from an understanding of the parts to an understanding of the whole (Michael C. Jackson, 2003). The challenge with looking into systems with this view is that the whole system is often not recognizable when looking at it in parts. The whole system is obviously affected by the relationships between the parts of the system, and as such, an alternative to reductionism has evolved, trying to look at the system as more than the sum of its parts. This study of systems is called holism.

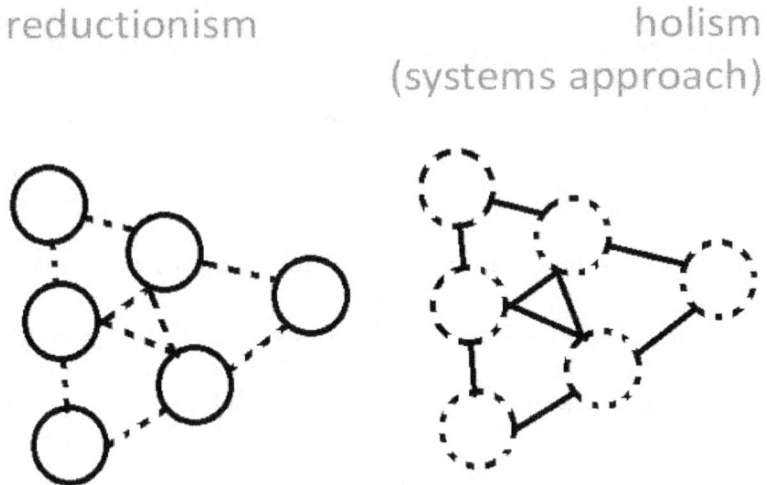

Figure 3. Reductionisms versus Holism.

We have to go back to the great philosophers like Aristotle and Plato to see the very start of the study of systems. Aristotle reasoned that the parts of the body only make sense in terms of the way they function to support the whole organism, and used this biological analogy to consider how individuals need to be related to the state. Whole organisms seemed to resist the attempts of scientific *reductionism* to reduce them to the sum of their parts. As a result, during the 1920s and 1930s, more *holistically* biologists began to argue that organisms were more than the sum of their parts. One of the best-known biologists who argued that organisms should be studied as complex wholes was Ludwig von Bertalanffy. He was the first biologist to publish an article on closed and open systems. While a closed system engages in no exchanges with its environment, an open system, such as an organism or an organization, has to interact with its environment to maintain itself in existence. Von Bertalanffy suggested that the sort of behaviour he witnessed in open systems in biology could be seen demonstrated by open systems in other domains. Soon, the general system theory was embraced by management thinkers who linked the open system model to their study of organizations. Another founding father of systems thinking, is Norbert Wiener, a mathematician and control engineer. He was interested in cybernetics, and argued that cybernetics was a new science that had application to many different disciplines because it dealt with laws that governed control processes, whatever the nature of the system under consideration. Cybernetics originally defined as *"the science of control and communication in the animal and the machine"*, was later redefined by Stafford Beer as *"the science of effective organization"*. Beer was determined to break with traditional management thinking. He looked at company organization charts and regarded them as unsatisfactory as a model for complex enterprises. They suggested that the person at the top of the organization needed a brain weighing half a ton – since all information flowed up to her and all decisions appeared to be her responsibility. In his study on cybernetics, he wanted to construct a more accurate and useful model, and the result was the *"viable system model"*. He used the human body as a model in his study to understand the behaviour of complex organizations. He argued that the human body is perhaps the richest and most flexible viable system of all. In his book, *Brain of the firm* (1972), Beer takes this example and builds a model consisting of five essential subsystems, which can be identified in the brain and body in line with major functional requirements. One of the most important findings of organizational cybernetics is that complex systems have a *"recursive"* nature. The organizational form of higher-level systems can be found repeated in the parts (Michael C. Jackson, 2003).

In a world of complexity and change, managers and workers are asked to tackle a much greater diversity of problems than was the case just a few decades ago. Today, managers and workers are looking for alternatives to their somewhat old methods of dealing with complex problems. In increasing numbers, they are turning toward systems thinking (Michael C. Jackson, 2003). Fundamentally, simple solutions fail because they are not holistic or creative enough. They are not holistic because they concentrate on the parts of the organization rather than the whole. In doing so they miss the crucial interactions between the parts. They fail to recognize that optimizing the performance of one part may have consequences for other parts of the system. This fault is known as "sub optimization".

So, how can the viable system model come in use for today's managers and workers in complex and ever-changing organizations? In short, the viable system model captures what it is like to view organizations as organisms with a brain. This is an extremely powerful way of thinking, which managers should treasure and employ as an alternative to the conventional model. In essence, the viable system model (VSM) is about the design of organizations as adaptive, goal-seeking entities. It pinpoints various systemic/structural laws that must be observed if an enterprise is to be viable and succeed (Michael C. Jackson, 2003). I will try to explain it here in my own words.

The starting point for the model is the concept of *variety*. It assumes that the environment surrounding the organization is of much greater variety than the organizations itself and that the organization is in turn of a much greater variety than the management. VSM is modelled with five systems in mind:

1. Implementation
2. Coordination
3. Operational control
4. Development
5. Policy

The *implementation system* (1) is of primary concern in the model, and is typically the core operational department within an organization (analogy to the muscles and organs in the human body). This system has to be as free as possible to deal with their environment, and have the autonomy needed to react to their environment in the best way possible. This is the most important system in the model, and system 2-5

are therefore called meta-systems. Without system 1, there would be no

need for system 2-5 - in fact, these systems are designed to facilitate

system 1.

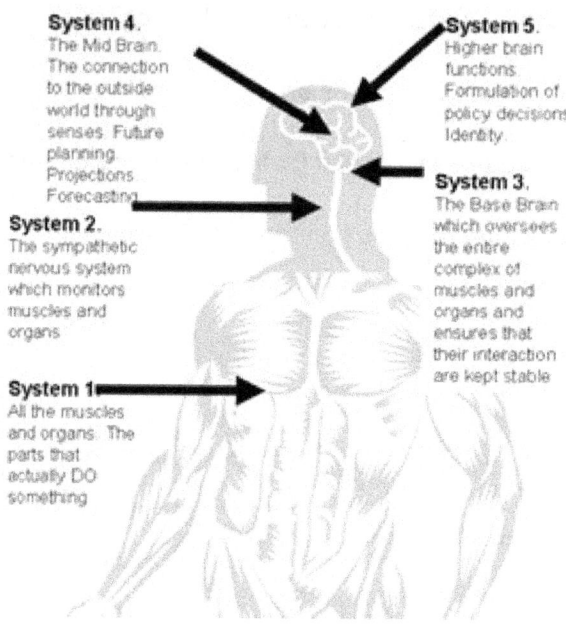

Figure 4. The Viable System Model – for the human body.

The *Coordination system* (2) is there to ensure harmony between

the elements of system 1 (analogy to the nervous system in the human

body). The *Operational control system* (3) functions as an operational

centre to supervise system 1, typically functions like human resources and finance (analogy to the base brain in the human body). It has overall

responsibility for the day-to-day running of the enterprise, trying its best

to ensure that policy is implemented appropriately. System 1, 2 and 3

together can maintain internal stability and optimize performance, within

an established framework, without reference to higher management.

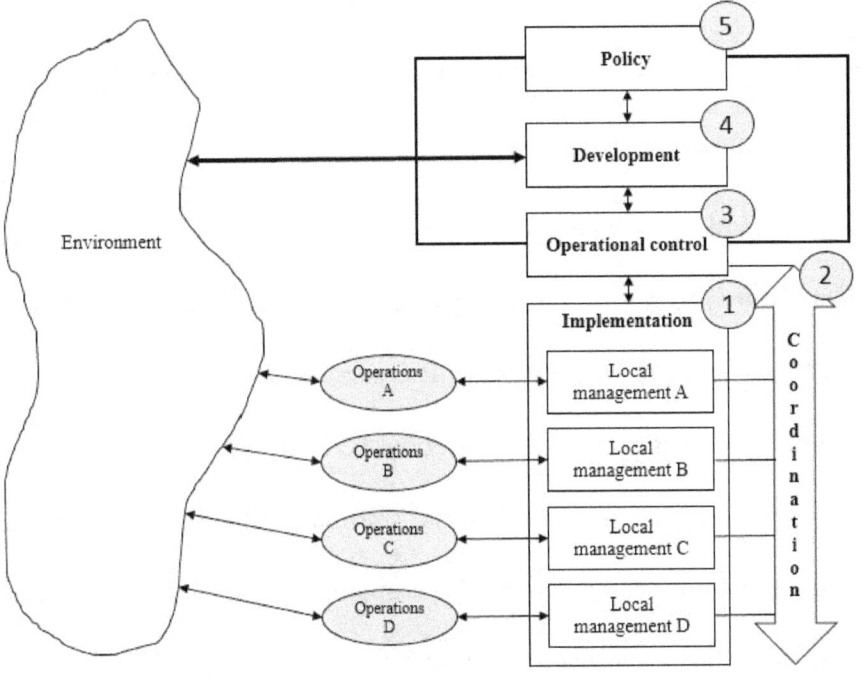

Figure 5. The Viable System Model – general model.

The *Development system* (4) is the operations room of the

organization – coupling information from internal operations with the variety within the environment of the organization (analogy to the mid brain in the human body). This is an environment for decision, and typically covers activities such as corporate planning, marketing, research and development. The *Policy system* (5) is responsible for the direction of the whole enterprise, and especially it has to balance the often-conflicting internal and external demands placed on the organization. This system must also articulate the identity and purposes of the whole system to the wider system of which it is part.

There is one final thing I need to say about Beer's work with the Viable System Model. And, reading it made me excited, because the same hypothesis has existed inside me I guess all through my adult career. The criteria for success for most organizations is measured in terms of money and profits. Beer argues that this is not satisfactory. It ignores how well the organization is doing in terms for preparing for the future by investing in research and development, or in terms of more abstract resources like employee morale. It fails to reveal the cost-cutting manager who, in search of immediate profit, is damaging the organization's long-term value. He also argues that the cost-cutting manager will increase productivity not by increasing actual achievement but by lowering capability (e.g., by neglecting research and development and employee morale) (Michael C. Jackson, 2003).

Creativity and Systems thinking

People who learn to read situations from different (theoretical) points of view have an advantage over those committed to a fixed position. For they are better able to recognise the limitations of a given perspective. They can see how situations and problems can be framed and reframed in different ways, allowing new kinds of solutions to emerge (Morgan, 1986). In my own words, these are the technology brokers. These are the people equipped with the special skills and networks making it possible to use existing technologies within one context, re-assemble them in slightly different ways, and make them useful in a new context.

It should be no surprise for any manager that different people within the organization will have different viewpoints, and that we most likely perceive the organization and the purpose of the organization in very different ways. Morgan (1986, 1997) has defined some familiar *metaphors*, which will help us to explore our own worldviews and to assist with creative thinking. Morgan defines eight metaphors in his study, and Michael C. Jackson has added the ninth metaphor from Alvesson and

Deetz, in his book *Systems Thinking - Creative Holism for managers*

(2003). Another way to look at the problem situations managers' face is to

view them from the perspectives offered by different sociological

paradigms. Paradigm refers to worldview or way of seeing things. Jackson

(2003) argues that it is possible to explain why creativity is best

encouraged if we embrace different paradigms as well as different

metaphors. In his book, *System Thinking – Creative Holism for managers*,

he also related these four paradigms to the nine metaphors. The

metaphors and the corresponding four common paradigms in use in social

theory today are listed in the figure below.

Metaphors	Short explanation	Common paradigms in social theory	Short explanation
Organizations as machines	A hierarchy of authority exercises coordination and control	The functionalist paradigm	It wants to ensure that everything in the system is functioning well so as to promote efficiency, adaption and survival.
Organizations as organisms	Looks at organizations as wholes made up of interrelated parts		
Organizations as brains	Emphasizes active learning rather than passive adaptability		
Organizations as flux and transformation	Asks managers to be less superficial in the way they read what is happening in their organizations		
Organizations as cultures	Successful managers should devote attention to the people associated with their organization and to the values, beliefs and philosophies held dear by those people	The interpretive paradigm	It believes social systems, such as organizations, result from the purposes people have and that these, in turn, stem from the interpretations they make of the situations in which they find themselves.
Organizations as political systems	Looks at how organizations are governed, at the pursuit and use of power and the micro politics of organizational life		
Organizations as psychic prisons	Emphasizes the impact it can have on the free development of our thinking	The emancipatory paradigm	It is concerned to "emancipate" oppressed individuals or groups in organizations and society. It is suspicious of authority and tries to reveal forms of power and domination that is sees as being illegitimately employed.
Organizations as instruments of domination	Shifts from the individual level of the psychic prisons to the group level and fixes attention on the way certain groups are exploiting others through organizations		
Organizations as carnivals	Normal order is suspended and creativity, diversity and ambivalence are encouraged.	The postmodern paradigm	Opposes the "modernist" rationality that is sees as present in all the other three paradigms.

Figure 6. System thinking metaphors and connected paradigms from social theory.

Throughout his book, Jackson (2003), explains different system approaches which falls into these categories:

- Improving Goal Seeking and Viability
- Exploring Purposes
- Ensuring Fairness
- Promoting Diversity

Bolman and Deal (2012) operates with similar metaphors or viewpoints in their book, *Reframing organizations. Artistry, Choice, and Leadership*; organization as a *factory*, organization as a *family*, organization as a *jungle*, and organization as a *temple or carnival*.

Metaphors	Short explanation	System approaches	Most commonly used approaches
Organizations as machines	A hierarchy of authority exercises coordination and control	Improving Goal Seeking and Viability	• Hard systems thinking • System dynamics • Organizational cybernetics • Complexity theory
Organizations as organisms	Looks at organizations as wholes made up of interrelated parts		
Organizations as brains	Emphasizes active learning rather than passive adaptability		
Organizations as flux and transformation	Asks managers to be less superficial in the way they read what is happening in their organizations		
Organizations as cultures	Successful managers should devote attention to the people associated with their organization and to the values, beliefs and philosophies held dear by those people	Exploring Purposes	• Strategic assumption surfacing and testing • Interactive planning • Soft systems methodology
Organizations as political systems	Looks at how organizations are governed, at the pursuit and use of power and the micro politics of organizational life		
Organizations as psychic prisons	Emphasizes the impact it can have on the free development of out thinking	Ensuring Fairness	• Critical systems heuristics • Team syntegrity
Organizations as instruments of domination	Shifts from the individual level of the psychic prisons to the group level and fixes attention on the way certain groups are exploiting others through organizations		
Organizations as carnivals	Normal order is suspended and creativity, diversity and ambivalence are encouraged.	Promoting Diversity	• Postmodern systems thinking

Figure 7. System thinking metaphors and connected system approaches.

The viable system model, which I described earlier, falls within the first category: *improving goal seeking and viability*. I will spare you for describing all of the system approaches mentioned in his book, but I will make my own conclusions and thoughts around the best approaches for dealing with the complex situations we face in organizations today in the next section.

Postmodern systems thinking & Creative Holism

Now, here is the funny thing. I was convinced when I started reading *Systems Thinking* (Jackson, 2003) that I would be first in line to give my support to the postmodern paradigm within system thinking, hence also to the system approaches within this paradigm. But, for some reason, as I continued to read about the postmodern paradigm and its philosophy, the only thing I could get out of it was the impression that this paradigm did nothing else but protest to all the other paradigms. And, they did so without really offering anything useful in return (because it would be inconsistent with the philosophy of postmodernism to offer a structured methodology for turning theory into practice). Postmodernists attack all the previous paradigms, and particularly the belief in rationality, truth and progress. Really? They deny that science can provide access to objective knowledge and so assist with steering organizations and societies in the face of complexity. Yes, you have understood it right; their suggestion is, to throw everything on the boat and let instability, disruption, disorder, contingency, paradox and chaos rule.

In all fairness, let me mention that the postmodern paradigm and its philosophers value diversity, complexity and creativity, but the lack of clear methodological guidance makes it difficult to get a good grasp on this paradigm and it methods and approaches in dealing with these complex problem situations.

Thank god for good endings, because in his book, Jackson (2003) concludes with the reference to *Total System Intervention* and *Critical Systems Thinking*, which is referred to as a dynamic metamethodology. Total system intervention is helping managers to advocate and enable the maximum creativity when the problem situation is being analysed, and to evaluate the usefulness of different management solutions, and particularly different systems approaches (Michael C. Jackson, 2003). It takes on holism, and opposes to a "one best way in all circumstances" mentality. The example referred to in his book, a case for North Yorkshire Police (NYP) in the mid 1990s, took TSI into use by using a varied set of

Morgan's (1986) "images" of organizations. Some of the common metaphors used by TSI are:

- Organization as machine

- Organization as organism

- Organization as brain

- Organization as culture

- Organization as coalition

- Organization as coercive system

There are three phases of the TSI metamethodology; *creativity*, *choice* and *implementation*. During the *creativity* phase, the task is to highlight the major concerns, issues and problems that exist in the problem context. Moreover, it is mandatory to use a wide range of different perspectives so that the picture built up of the problem situation is derived from viewing it from different paradigms. During the second phase, the *choice* phase, the task is to construct a suitable intervention strategy around the choice of systems methodology or combination of systems methodologies. During the third phase, the *implementation* phase, the task is to employ the selected systems methodology or methodologies with a view to bringing about positive change. It is usual to end up with one methodology being deemed dominant; however, TSI will always want to ensure that other methodologies are also included in the analysis of the problem situation to broaden the focus and to always include soft systems methodologies. As for the example with NYP, the *Viable System Model* was used to help interpret the problem situation from a brain perspective. It was chosen as the dominant approach, but they also included *Interactive Planning* as a second methodology to assist in the problem analysis and implementation phase (Michael C. Jackson, 2003, p. 293).

The relevance

The reason for bringing systems thinking into the topic of dealing with change is that the world is becoming more complex. Our products and services are becoming more complex, the way we perform our day-to-day work is becoming more complex, and our organizations are becoming more complex. From systems thinking theory we have learned that a more holistic view is needed to see the structures that underlie complex situations. What I am trying to achieve with this is a means to understand the behaviour of complex organizations. To succeed with change in disruptive times it is my personal belief that a more adaptive approach is needed. Systems thinking and the holistic views therein should be useful for most organization, and it will help them in adapting to the changing business environment.

Are we doing the right things?

Introduction

"There is no one right way or 'one size fits all' approach to portfolio management."

The following topics are covered in this chapter:

- Types of demand in an organization
- Portfolio management
- Benefits of Portfolio management
- Resource/Capacity management
- Project prioritization
- Governance models
- Strategic planning
- Portfolio definition cycle

Different types of demand

We can generally describe demand using three broad categories (Taming Change, 2010, p. 69):

- **Base services** represent the continuum of level-of-effort work needed to deliver existing products and services at current production and quality levels, and to generally maintain the supporting assets and operations of your organization.
- **Strategic initiatives** are major changes of operational significance. Typically, this class of demand constitutes the portfolio of formally managed projects, including new product development.
- **Other planned work** constitutes the organizational demands that fall in between base services and strategic initiatives. This includes shorter-term activities that are beyond level-of-effort operations such as noncapital maintenance and enhancement projects; emerging major break-fix activities, and making incremental, evolutionary improvements.

As a general rule, organizations find that about half of their demand falls within the base services category, whit the remaining amount roughly split between strategic initiatives and other planned work. Almost every organization has a grasp on its strategic work. Even the most basic and informally managed organizations usually has a defined project list and a governing body to manage it. I will discuss the tools, processes and best practices for this more in depth in the following pages.

What is less certain though is whether most organizations can see and clearly understand other planned work in measurable terms. Too often, an organization can suffer from a large volume of informal assignments and requests passing between managers and departments, and also, between co-workers. These activities are often hard to manage and control. This is typically when demand and capacity management in many organizations runs into trouble. Other planned work activities do not get sufficient attention, because either management teams don't understand the total effort of such demands, or even more likely, because they don't see a reason to work structured with activities within this category. And, they might be right.

Portfolio management

Portfolio management is a set of disciplined processes for making smart business decisions about change events. The main question being: *are we doing the right things?* The objectives of portfolio management are to ensure:

- The change initiatives that are being delivered (and those in the development pipeline) represent the *optimum allocation* of resources in the context of the organization's strategic objectives, available resources and risk or achievability.
- The portfolio is *sufficient* to achieve the desired contribution to strategic objectives.
- All initiatives are *necessary* to achieve the desired contribution to strategic objectives.
- The selected change initiatives are delivered effectively and cost-efficiently.
- All the potential benefits are realized.

Four broad types of management information are pivotal to the decisions you make about change event (Taming Change, 2010, p. 35):

- People
- Money
- Work
- Deliverables

People and money represent the primary capacities that you have, and should be considered your main focus when making business decisions. Although these two capacities have nothing physically in common, they share an important relationship that is so obvious that it is completely missed by most organizations. Everyone understands the need to rigorously manage financial resources – organizations often go to great lengths and levels of detail to be sure they do so. The CFO and accounting organization dedicate themselves to managing the general ledger, balance sheets, credit and debits, accounts receivable, and various budgets. Other executives spend a good portion of their energy on financial governance. The entire management team usually participates in the budgeting process.

The imperative for applying meticulous financial controls is due in part to the fungible nature of money; it is highly transportable, a universally accepted commodity, and convertible to practically anything else, including other forms of capacity.

However, people perform work. In knowledge-driven organizations, people represent the primary raw material used to create value. As a result, a significant percentage of financial capacity goes toward acquiring, paying, and enabling staff and contracted resources. If you are in an organization that relies on its highly skilled group of professionals as the prime means of creating products and services (typically technical service organizations), chances are that over half of your operating expenses relate somehow to your resources. Yet, despite these relationships between people and money, one compelling difference between them elevates the priority of effective resource management (Taming Change, 2010, p. 80).

Resource and Capacity Management

You can put excess money in the safe or suspend payments, but the effort of your people cannot be stored or put on hold. Like water over the dam, every hour of effort passed through your organization is in constant flow. Whether you direct it productively or not; once it has passed, it is irretrievable. If a change event disrupts your organization and creates confusion among the staff, you cannot simply turn off the flow of effort until you figure it out.

With all of this in mind, it does not make sense to go to great measures to manage money unless you apply a similar level of diligence and governance to manage the effort of your organization. Yet, this is often a common situation in organizations, small and large.

The fundamental advantage of portfolio management lies in how it enables you to address the demands placed on your organization so that you can produce the greatest value with the capacities that you have available (Taming Change, 2010, p. 81). In order to achieve this greater level of match between demand and capacity, you will need to implement and establish governance processes concerned with resource and capacity management.

Even though the situation is slightly different from organization to organization, we can nevertheless assume that most companies divide their demands in the three categories as outlined in the beginning of this chapter; *base services*, *strategic initiatives* and *other planned work*. Resource capacity planning establishes a capacity allocation plan that takes into account the following inputs (Taming Change, 2010, p. 147):

- Ongoing operational demands of the organization (base services)
- Current in-progress projects and initiatives and their future capacity needs
- Additional strategic initiatives proposed by operational planning
- Other anticipated demands over the planning horizon (future emerging initiatives and other planned work)

- Relative timing of these demands and their capacity consumption rates

- Current resource capacity and utilization

- Capacity sourcing options and the cost of capacity

The ideal mechanism for gathering historical capacity information is to report effort expended on individual work activities. Time reporting provides the summary level information needed for capacity planning. If no form of time reporting information is available, you may have to rely on some other form of non-labor information to extrapolate an estimate of capacity utilization.

Leadership has another level at its disposal to manage capacity – timing. As new objectives or strategies are identified, the natural tendency is, "Hurry up! Let's get this done as soon as possible!". Sounds familiar, right? However, near-term availability is often scarce or non-existent. Governing bodies may need to consider slowing down, spreading out, or rearranging how the total portfolio of initiatives is slated for execution.

Decision to pursue change initiatives with external resources or service providers is yet another capacity management lever. If a strategy represents work that is outside the capabilities of existing staff, then the "build versus buy" discussion might conclude that it is faster, less expensive, and less risky to contract that work out rather than perform it in-house. One should also consider how this change initiative pursued with in-house efforts would happen at the expense of other ongoing projects and change initiatives.

From my own experience, I have found it useful to start with a lightweight resource and capacity management model. Do not start by searching the internet for resource management tools. Please…. An Excel sheet will do for quite a while. Take a resource-centric approach, and focus primarily on the departments, divisions or other group of resources that is heavily involved in project work. Start by getting an overview of the resources, along with the percentage of their time available for change initiatives (project work). Being realistic in defining the percentage for change is crucial here. Research has shown that in modern organizations, formally managed projects typically constitute an average of 15 percent to 30 percent of the total workload. A good portion of the workforce has ongoing operational responsibilities in addition to specific project tasks that often spans multiple initiatives. And, remember, many project managers and other leaders are not trained to understand the complexities of the modern knowledge worker environment. Then, it is time to allocate their time between the ongoing projects and being sure that resources are allocated based on project priority. If you don't have the prioritization in place when working with resource and capacity management, you will soon realize that a crucial piece of the puzzle is missing. Unless the projects are ranked/prioritized, the typical knowledge worker will have the tendency to choose the project tasks that seems most interesting from a competence point of view. Who wouldn't? It will be a much easier job for the department manager to supervise the knowledge workers activities when the management team has clearly stated the ranked prioritization of the change initiatives currently running.

When this is in place, it is also easy to see how many projects you realistically can deliver with the current capacity and resource setup. If the capacity within the organization only allows you to work on 6 out of 10 top priority projects, management need to know where the capacity bottlenecks are, and what alternatives they have to remedy the situation.

Project prioritization process

There are many levels of maturity when it comes to portfolio management, and there are different models available to measure, document and improve maturity levels within the organization. One such model is the P3M3 (Axelos), which is a portfolio, programme and project management maturity model. In my experience, one of the most fundamental areas to improve on in the area of portfolio management is the project prioritization process. If that process is non-existing within your organization, it becomes extremely difficult for anyone working with change initiatives to secure sufficient project resources, senior management commitment and all other means necessary to secure timely deliveries and overall progress in your project. Nothing is more demotivating than working in a project which seem to have low priority, and which constantly is getting affected by surrounding projects or business as usual activities being considered as more urgent and with higher priority. This also goes hand-in-hand with resource and capacity management processes. Without having insights into which resources are scarce resources for change initiatives across the organization, you will never be able to perform a proper project prioritization process either. Not surprisingly, this becomes even more difficult when you find yourself in a technical service organization, where knowledge workers constitutes your primary capacity.

Multitasking is a relevant topic to mention when we start talking about projects and prioritization processes. Technical service organizations are synonymous with multi-tasking. The majority of today's knowledge workers are simultaneously assigned to several different work activities with varying duration. With each transition from one assignment to the next, individuals lose productive time. Experience from Durbin and Doerscher (Taming change, 2010) indicates that stops and starts alone consume 15 percent or more of the total availability of people who are trying to make progress on several different unrelated tasks per day. In addition, there is the constant interruptions often present in work environments. One study suggests that on average 28 percent of working time is consumed by phone calls, new e-mail notifications, doorway conversations, and similar disruptions. To maximize results, managers should strive to limit the number of tasks simultaneously assigned.

We recently implemented a project prioritization process at my current employer, and the benefits of doing so have been surprisingly many. Up until this point, we had assumed that we had the capacity within our organization to perform 20 projects in parallel across the portfolio: Project Quote phase (5), Project Foundation phase (5), and Project Execution phase (10). Even though we had an impression of the scarce resources, we could never really argue with facts when these discussions came up at management level. Therefore, a prioritization process was implemented, to secure a more optimal use of resources (read: knowledge workers).

The first benefit we experienced with the new process was a common understanding of the overall goals and priorities of the organization. The management team was given the task to reconsider the rank of top 10 projects in every weekly management team meeting. This led to an updated rank of top 10 projects distributed in various forums and meetings across the organization. Line managers clearly saw benefits of having a *"clear sight"* into organizations goals, and by allocating resources based on the top 10 rank of projects, they felt more confident that the resources were utilized in a more optimal way than before.

Secondly, the top 10 rank of projects is now communicated throughout the organization, which triggers a completely new set of intelligence for the wider organization. It is easier to see how operational activities are connected to the projects (change initiatives) and how and why resources are allocated in terms of meeting the goals of the organization.

The last benefit, probably not worth mentioning, is the importance of the prioritization process seen in connection with the resource and capacity management. Whenever a project within top 10 is completed, resources are allocated to the next project in line (within top 10). The level of resource bargaining with line managers (well known for project managers) has drastically reduced. There is an increased clarity for all the relevant managers and personnel involved in change initiatives, which projects should get resources and in which sequence. The resource and capacity management process, in turn, has made it possible to identify resource/competence bottlenecks, and remedies are agreed to reduce these bottlenecks.

As in every other part of dealing with change, nothing comes for free. You have to be sure that your organization has the personnel available to drive both the project prioritization process and the connected resource and capacity management process. These processes go hand in hand, and must be visible all the way up to the management team (executive level).

Benefits of Portfolio Management

The ultimate goal of portfolio management is to tame change by providing a proven discipline for delivering value through informed decision-making (Taming Change, 2010, p. 45).

Pat Durbin and Terry Doerscher's (Taming Change, 2010) focus on three critical characteristics of the portfolio management discipline that leverage its power in taming change:

- *Transparency*: The goal and methods of reaching decisions are available for all participants to see. While individuals may not always agree with them, business objectives are clearly documented and communicated.
- *Discipline*: Strict adherence to consistent and proven methods that apply a systematic, quantified analysis approach avoids venturing into personality-driven dead ends and alerts decision makers to opportunities that might otherwise go unnoticed.
- *Trustworthiness*: Each person involved in the process understands how decisions are made. Trusting the process becomes a critical component in each person's proactive

commitment to implement the decision. Performance towards goals is communicated to everyone.

The extension of portfolio management across an organization allows multiple users in different roles to view common information in different ways:

- **Executives** use portfolios to set goals, develop strategies, govern the organization, control capacities, and monitor performance.
- **Financial managers** use portfolios to link budgets and funding to segments by demographics, geography, product lines, and so on.
- **Investment managers** have portfolios of investment opportunities.
- **Product managers** have portfolios of products or services.
- **Resource managers** have portfolios of staff by skill, location, or role.
- **Program/project managers** have portfolios of projects.
- **Portfolio management offices** support and facilitate alignment throughout the organization and provide common portfolio management methods and tools.

While it is common for most organizations to use multiple portfolios, remember that the ultimate goal of portfolio management is to provide a unified view of change events from many different perspectives.

When taking capacity management into the portfolio management equation, it is crucial to ask yourself this vital question: do the current change initiatives represent the *optimum allocation* of resources in the context of the organization's strategic objectives, available resources and risk or achievability? Remember, the effort of your people cannot be stored or put on hold. It is a sign of project and portfolio management maturity whenever management (be it project directors or other governing bodies within an organization) can demonstrate that changes are needed in the portfolio or within the capacity side to meet the stated strategic goals.

Let me give you an example of this. I used to work for a debt collection company. In my role as Head of PMO, one of my functions was to provide governance and frameworks for project and portfolio management for all IT projects within all business unit. Due to low maturity in portfolio management especially, I encouraged the chairpersons of each portfolio management committee to start looking at projects that no longer were supporting the strategic agenda. To emphasize the importance of this, I actually promised a bottle of Champagne to the first person that stepped up and suggested to terminate a project, which did not represent the optimum allocation of resources in the context of strategic objectives and available resources. When this finally happened, I gave the chairperson a bottle of Champagne and told him that this was a sign of maturity and that he should never stop asking this crucial question about optimizing the portfolio. Off course, everyone else thought I was crazy. No one should encourage anyone to terminate a project before it is finalized right? I am afraid that the easy answer to this is, yes, of course you should!

How to succeed with Portfolio management?

To be able to succeed with portfolio management there are certain principles that holds true for any organization. These principles provide the organizational environment in which the portfolio definition and delivery practices can operate effectively. These principles are shown in the figure below:

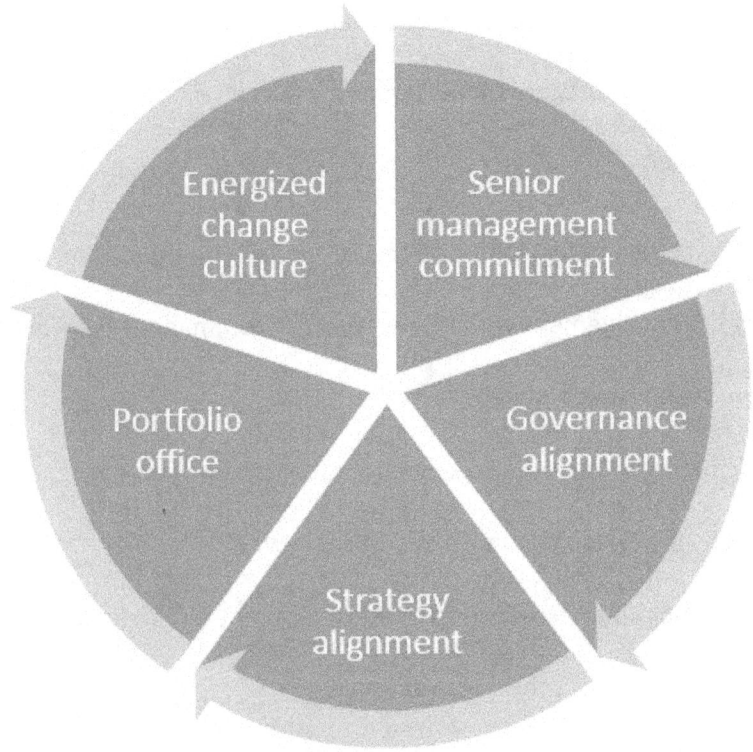

Figure 8. The five principles of Portfolio Management.

These principles cannot easily be prioritized, but without **senior management commitment**, you have a long way ahead. It might make sense to you, but if the rest of the organization do not see the benefit of having these processes in place, you will need some serious patience in trying to implement this. The first job for you is to get the management on board. Easy? No. A necessity? Yes. Proactive and visible senior management commitment is identified repeatedly in academic and industry research as being absolutely essential to effective portfolio management. Senior managers should support portfolio management in the following ways:

- Publicly championing and positively communicating the value of portfolio management within their areas of command – especially when the going gets tough.

- Participating in decision-making about the composition of the portfolio in a personal, active and positive way.

- Contributing their expertise to the development of portfolio management across the organization.

- Taking effective steps to ensure compliance with portfolio governance and prevent pet projects from being progressed under the "radar".

- Explaining the rationale for decisions to their staff.

- Personally demonstrating the behaviours essential to the success of portfolio management – senior managers must actually do what they say in taking a portfolio-wide rather than departmental perspective.

Any organization has some *__governance__* model in place for the wider organizational structure. The same goes for portfolio management. There has to be clarity as to what decisions are made, where and by whom, and what criteria are used in reaching these decisions. Effective portfolio governance also means that the governance of the portfolio needs to reflect, and be consistent with, the wider organizational governance model. There might be a single decision-making body, or there might be a two-board structure for decision-making. The relationship between portfolio management boards and other relevant boards should be documented in the portfolio management framework so that everyone is clear about who is responsible and accountable for what and to whom.

The relationship between portfolio management and *__strategy__* is two-way – strategic objectives provide the context within which portfolio management operates; the latter provides a means to engage the change delivery functions in the development and delivery of that strategy and in due course provides evidence on the successful implementation of strategy. As the strategic alignment is at the very core of portfolio management, I will dive more into this later in this chapter.

Portfolio management enables the relevant portfolio governance bodies to make better and more informed investment decisions. A function is therefore required to provide timely and accurate information to facilitate that decision-making process. Different organizations have different names on this function, but for now, let us call it the *portfolio office*. The key services provided by the portfolio office are:

- Defining portfolio-wide PPM standards, processes and templates to ensure consistent approaches are applied and to provide clear line of sight across the portfolio.

- Providing an assurance to senior management on effective and efficient management and delivery of change initiatives.

- Providing a challenge or critical-friend role for individual initiatives.

- Providing support, advice and guidance to individual change initiatives – whilst ensuring that this does not compromise the portfolio office's independence from the delivery functions by, for example, ensuring different staff provide the support and assurance/challenge functions.

- Preparing the portfolio strategy and delivery plan.

- Coordinating and participating in stage/phase gate, investment appraisal, portfolio-level prioritization and progress reviews.

- Preparing the portfolio dashboard.

- Improving the links and feedback loop between policy and strategy formulation and PPM delivery.

A portfolio office is not simply a bigger programme or project office. In summary, portfolio offices differ from programme and project offices in the following ways. While programme and project offices are primarily concerned with coordinating the delivery of individual change initiatives in the right way, portfolio offices are concerned with ensuring these initiatives remain strategically aligned, coordinating delivery at a collective level, monitoring benefits realization, and ensuring that senior management receive relevant and timely information on the performance of the portfolio. Also, while programme and project offices are temporary structures set up to support a specific change initiative, portfolio offices are usually permanent and integrated into the organizational governance structure. Ideally, they should have direct contact with, and report to, the management board.

I do not think I can emphasize the last principle, *energized change culture*, enough – because success with change and innovation can only truly be realized if the people working for the organization are engaged, focused on the appropriate goals, and feel a sense of working together as one team. An energized change culture includes elements such as:

- Senior management commitment, communication and motivation.

- A mutual and shared desire to succeed based on effective employee engagement.

- Effective governance with an appropriate level of bureaucracy.

- Culture and behaviours reflective of a focus on the overall good and success of the organization rather than individual or silo-based interest.

Strategic planning

As mentioned earlier, *strategy* is the very core of portfolio management. Strategic planning therefore sets the context within which portfolio management operates by providing:

- The basis for determining the scope of the portfolio and the prioritization of individual initiatives.

- The measure against which portfolio management will ultimately be assessed, i.e. whether or not the changes to the business have helped the organization achieve its strategic objectives.

Wikipedia defines strategic planning as *an organization's process of defining its strategy, or direction, and making decisions on allocating its resources to pursue this strategy.* As part of strategic planning, portfolio management addresses four fundamental questions:

1. Are the programmes and projects in our portfolio *necessary* in the context of our strategic objectives?

2. Is our portfolio, together with business as usual activities, *sufficient* to achieve our strategic objectives?

3. Is the overall level of risk acceptable and is the portfolio of initiatives *achievable*?

4. Is the portfolio *affordable* – and if not, which initiatives should be dropped or re-scheduled?

The literature around strategy and strategic planning is massive, and I will not step my foot in to the endless processes and methods available for strategic planning. I will nevertheless stress the crucial task for any management team, in bringing strategy into portfolio management processes. Unless there is a clear vision for the company, and hence a clear strategic direction with clear goals for the organization, portfolio management becomes a very struggle some activity. Aligning change initiatives to strategic objectives can best be achieved via benefits, i.e. by expressing the benefits anticipated from change initiatives in terms consistent with the organization's strategic objectives and targets (for example, improved turnover, customer satisfaction, cost per unit etc.). This in turn depends on change initiatives having a reliable business case – not necessarily a long document, but one that demonstrates clearly the business drivers, benefits and the factors affecting their achievability. The benefits should be indentified in sufficient and consistent detail to enable their contribution to the strategic measures to be assessed and compared with other potential investments.

A typical problem organizations can face is that their strategic objectives are set at such a high level that determining the contribution of individual change initiatives to the strategic direction is difficult. One solution is to develop a driver-based model where the implicit logic underpinning the strategic objectives is made explicit. The figure below illustrates how benefits from change initiatives align with strategic objectives. It also identifies a change initiative that is not linked to a strategic objective and which should therefore be reviewed as to whether it should continue or stop. The fundamental question to ask in such situations is whether the organization has free capacity to allocate resources to such change initiatives, or whether resources are scarce and should be re-allocated to change initiatives supporting stated strategic objectives instead.

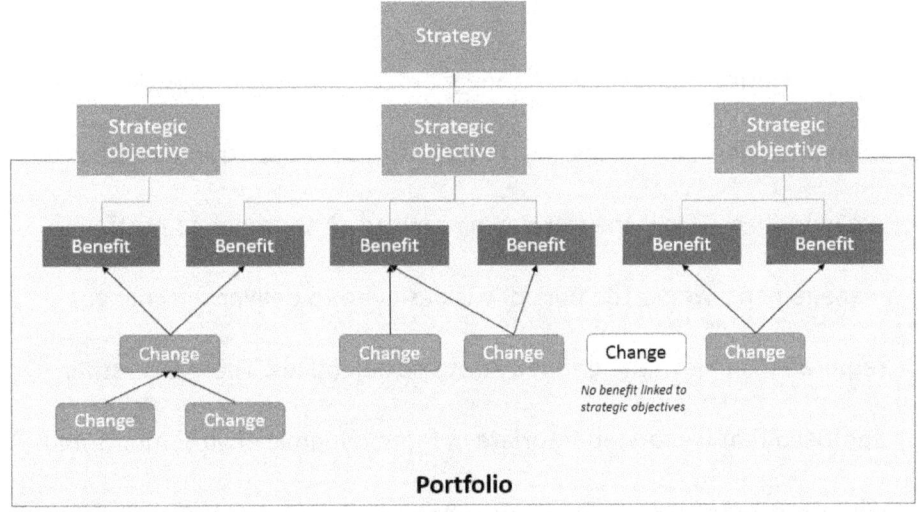

Figure 9. Alignment of change initiatives with strategic objectives.

Portfolio definition cycle

The Axelos global best practice joint venture has defined five practices found within the portfolio definition cycle, and they are:

- Understand

- Categorize

- Prioritize

- Balance

- Plan

During the strategic planning process, strategic objectives are developed and the changes needed to achieve those strategic objectives are identified. This is the top-down or strategic approach to portfolio management, where the portfolio is designed to deliver the changes required to achieve the defined strategic objectives. There is another approach that is more appropriate in more dynamic environments and where strategy is emergent – here change initiative are proposed bottom-up and are appraised and prioritized on a regular basis in the context of the current high-level strategic objectives. Whichever approach is adopted, top-down or bottom-up, the purpose of the **understand** practice is the same – to obtain a clear and transparent view of what is in the current portfolio and the project development pipeline, performance to date and, looking forward, the forecast costs, benefits, and risks to delivery and benefits realization (MoP, Axelos, 2013).

Categorization organizes change initiatives into groups, segments or sub-portfolios based on the strategic objectives or other groupings as required. The investment criteria used to appraise and prioritize initiatives can be tailored to suit the specific category or segment. The purpose of the *categorize* practice is to make it easier for senior decision makers to understand the make-up of their portfolio and thus to make decisions on balance and on the optimum use of available funding and other resources.

Prioritizing ranks the change initiatives within the portfolio (or portfolio segment) based on one or more agreed measures. The most common measures are financial metrics and/or some form of multi-criteria analysis. The purpose of the *prioritize* practice is to help senior management (and the portfolio governance body) answer the following questions – subject to considerations of an appropriate balance between risk and return:

- Which initiatives should the organization invest in?

- What are the most important initiatives?

- What initiatives must be resourced above all others?

Prioritization results in a ranked list of strategic changes. The purpose of the **balance** practice is to ensure that the resulting portfolio is balanced in terms of factors such as timing, coverage of all strategic objectives, impact across the business, stage of initiative development, overall risk, return profile, and available resources.

The purpose of the **plan** practice is to collate information from the portfolio definition cycle and create a portfolio strategy and delivery plan, which will be approved by the portfolio governing body.

Are we doing them right?

Introduction

"Although the conventional project management body of knowledge forms a good foundation for basic training and initial learning, it may not suffice for addressing the complex problems of today's projects (Shenhar & Dvir, 2007)."

The following topics are covered in this chapter:

- How Now - Brown Cow
- Strategic Project Leadership
- Diamond approach
- Failure and success criteria's for projects
- Seven Key's to success

Project Management

Are we doing them right? This question is only relevant after having answered the most critical question in handling change initiatives and portfolio management, namely: Are we doing the right things? Let's say that your organization has done the homework, and have picked the right change initiatives (projects) to fulfil the strategic agenda, and is ready to start executing. How should we, as project managers, be sure that we are *doing them right*? It is a very intricate question, and I am afraid there is no straightforward, out of the box, answer to that. However, there are some tricks to it. From my background as a project manager, and as a line manager providing mentoring to other project managers, I have used a few very good methods to be more certain that the project is actually doing the right things. Let us first look at a method called *Brown Cow*.

How Now - Brown Cow

The *Brown Cow* is a method developed by The Atlantic Systems Guild, and is available at Volere (http://volere.co.uk). A common problem voiced by requirements analysts is: *"people don't tell me their requirements; they tell me a solution to some unstated problem"*. This focus on solutions is further complicated when it is mixed together with current business constraints, technical constraints and personal perceptions of the world. The Brown Cow model is a tool for helping to understand a number of different viewpoints in parallel.

Typically useful systems viewpoints are *Now* (often referred to as "as is") and *Future* (also called "to be"). The Brown Cow takes a more granular approach by looking at the *How* (solution) and *What* (essence) of both Now and Future. Figure 3 is a generic model that illustrates the sorts of subject matter you might identify as belonging to each of the four points of view. Each of the quadrants focuses on a specific point of view and provides you with a way of organizing what you discover.

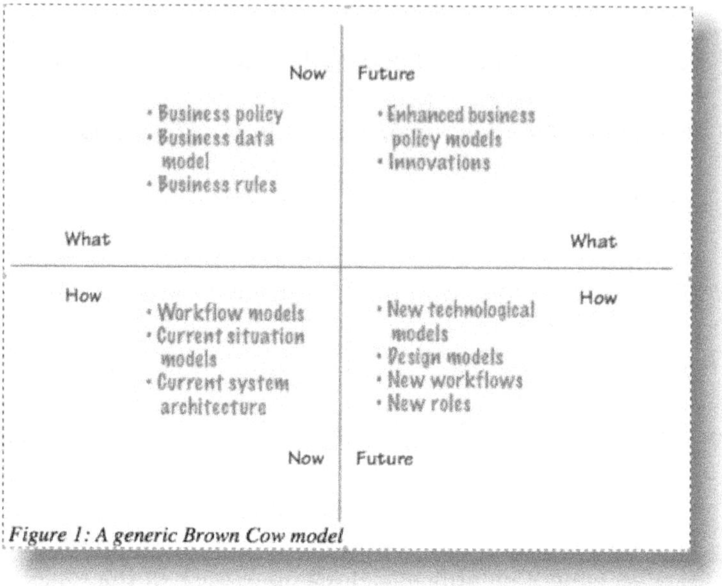

Figure 10. A Generic Brown Cow model

As an example of practical use, we made our own model of this, and named the quadrants (starting at lower left) for *AS-IS*, *Headache*, *Target*, and *Design*. As you can see from the figure below, the *AS-IS* situation is derived from How/Now, and the *Headache* situation is derived from and What/Now (unless you are experiencing a headache in What/Now, there isn't really a need to change anything, is it?). The *Target* situation is derived from What/Future, and finally the *Design* situation is derived from the How/Future.

This proved to be a simple, yet very powerful method, to get a better understanding of the real problem and the different viewpoints across different stakeholders for a specific project. After only 1 hour of facilitated work going through the specific headache for the project, it became very clear for the resources involved what the *complete* headache was as of today, and what was needed in the future to meet the target situation we all agreed upon. As such, this method is very powerful in assuring that the complete scope of the project is taken into account, and also, that all resources involved get a better understanding of the other stakeholders' needs and viewpoints.

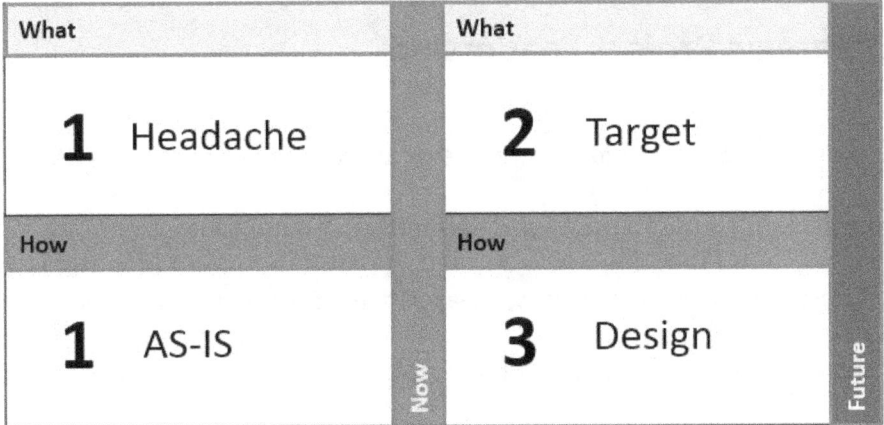

Figure 11. Brown Cow model

Quite often, we experienced that the preliminary solution (already sold in at the management level) was either the wrong solution, the right solution - but for the wrong problem, or not a complete solution to meet the stated target situation.

There are many ways of looking at any problem. Trying to think of everything at once results in misunderstandings, missed questions and missed opportunities. The Brown Cow model provides a tool for taking four important systems viewpoints in parallel. The non-procedural nature of the model means that the analyst can choose to take the most relevant viewpoints in whatever order suits the particular situation.

Strategic Project Leadership

When is a project considered a success? Every project needs more than one dimension for assessing success, and those dimensions vary from project to project. First, success measures must reflect the strategic agenda of the company and its business objectives for three reasons (Shenhar & Dvir, 2007):

1. If a project does not serve the organization, why do it at all?

2. It should encompass success at different times: what may seem well done in the short run may end later in disappointment, and short-term setbacks may turn into long-term rewards.

3. Success measures should reflect the interests of various stakeholders who will be affected by the project's outcome.

Reflecting on this list, it is obvious that methods like Brown Cow, will increase the possibilities of success for any project out there.

Diamond approach

It is time to explain the diamond approach more in detail. The diamond approach offers a disciplined tool for assessing a project's benefits and risks and for selecting the right project management style. It also gives you a model for assessing a project at midcourse, and for putting a troubled project back on track. The diamond model includes four dimensions (as previously mentioned) to distinguis among projects: novelty, technology, complexity, and pace. The diamond approach is shown in the figure below.

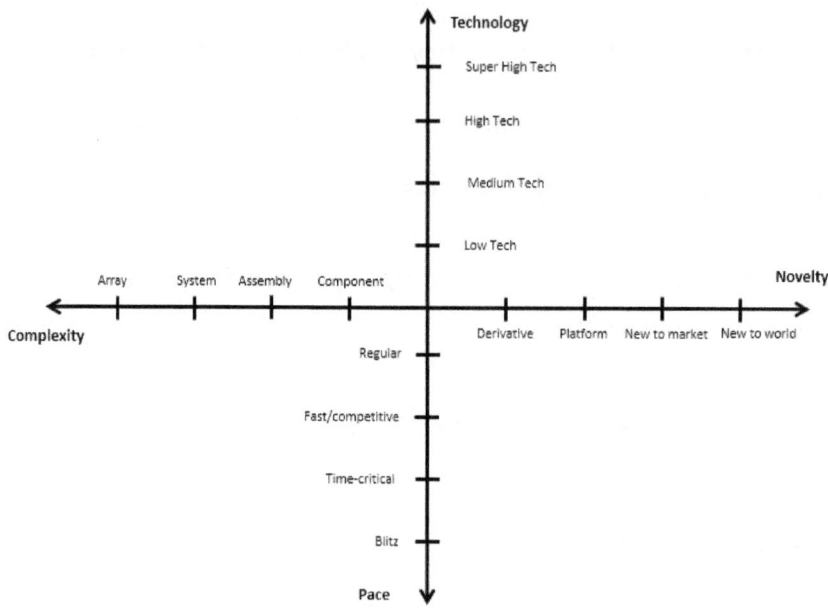

Figure 12. The Diamond approach (Shenhar and Dvir, 2007).

Every project manager knows this, but I think it is safe to say that we need to constantly remind ourselves that *every project is unique*. They can be distinguished by technology, size, risk, environment, customer, contract, complexity, skills, geography, and many more aspects. However, projects also have a lot in common. Every project has a goal, limited time and other resources, and a project manager or leader, and projects typically develop budgets, schedules, and organizations to determine who does what. The question is how to combine the common and the different elements into one model that allows managers to classify their projects and choose the right approach for each project.

Shenhar and Dvir (2007) undertook extensive research to understand the underlying dimensions that make one project different from, or similar to, another in ways that could tell us how to manage projects more effectively. Drawing on classic contingency theory, they concluded that they could define three dimensions that characterize each project: uncertainty, complexity, and pace. *Uncertainty* refers to the state of our information about the project's goal, its task, and its environment; often this information is sketchy and incomplete, especially at the outset. *Complexity* is a measure of the project scope, reflected in characteristics such as the number of tasks and the degree of interdependency between them. And, of course, *pace* relates to the time dimension and the existence of "soft" or "hard" deadlines that drive the work (Shenhar & Dvir, 2007, p. 41). Going further with their research, they soon realized that there were in fact two sources of uncertainty; market uncertainty, and technological uncertainty. Hence, emerged the model with the four distinctive dimensions; *novelty, technology, complexity*, and *pace*.

Novelty

Now, let us go into each dimension at a time. Novelty is the dimension concerned with *how new the product is to its markets and potential users.* The dimension represents the extent to which customers are familiar with this kind of product, the way to use it, and its benefits.

Derivative
Derivative products are extensions and improvements of existing products.

Platform
Platform products are new generations of existing product lines. Such products replace previous products in a well-established market sector. A typical example is a new car model.

New to the market
Taking an existing product into a new market to a new set of customers. The first commercial GPS is a good example of this.

New to the world
Such products are new-to-the-world. They transform a new concept or a new idea into a new product that customers have never seen before. The first Sony Walkman and the first 3M Post-it notes are typical examples.

Figure 13. Diamond approach - Novelty dimension.

Managers must understand these differences and adapt their managerial activities to the project's novelty level. For example, for *platform* projects, companies should perform extensive market research, study the data of previous generations, and carefully plan product prices. The story is quite different when it comes to *breakthrough* projects *(new-to-the-world)*. We distinguished earlier in this book between incremental and radical innovation. Radical innovation represents a diversion from known markets and known solutions or technologies, whereas incremental innovation seeks to build on, complement, and extend existing products. Radical innovation does not build and extend what exists, but rather seeks to overturn it. It is sometimes destructive to the skills, practices, product forms, and social relationships that exist within an organization (Shenhar & Dvir, 2007, p. 67). Hence, marketing of *new-to-the-world* products is different from marketing of the other three types. It is focused on getting the attention of customers. Its goal is to educate customers about the potential of the new product and often to articulate hidden customer needs.

Technology

Technological uncertainty represent the major source of task uncertainty. Technological uncertainty has an impact on, among other things, design and testing, communication and interaction, the timing of design freeze, and the needed number of design cycles. It also affects the technical competence needed by the project manager and project team members (Shenhar & Dvir, 2007, p. 47).

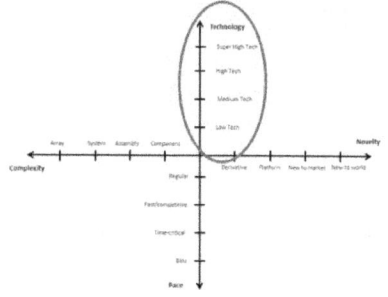

Low-tech
Projects rely on existing and well-established technologies. The most typical examples are construction projects.

Medium-tech
Projects which use mainly existing or base technologies but incorporate a new technology or a new feature that did not exist in previous products.

High-tech
These projects represent situations in which most of the technologies employed are new to the firm but already exist and are available at project initiation. Most computer and defense development projects belong to this category.

Super-high-tech
Projects in this category are based on new technologies that do not exist at project initiation. Although the mission is clear, the solution is not, and new technologies must be developed during the project.

Figure 14. Diamond approach - Technology dimension.

Managers should consider a project's level of technological uncertainty during the planning and organizing phase. They should schedule the design freeze and the number of design cycles based on technological uncertainty, as well as contingent resources, technical peer reviews, and the technical competence of the team (Shenhar & Dvir, 2007, p. 100).

Complexity

Complexity represent the system scope, and usually a lower scope level can be seen as a subsystem of the next higher level. Project complexity is directly related to system scope and affects project organization and the formality of project management. Although project complexity depends greatly on the complexity of the product (or outcome) of the project, note

that this dimension focuses on the complexity of the *project*, not the

product.

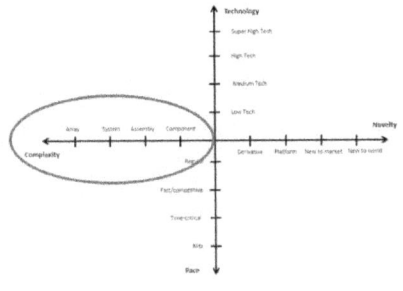

Component

A component represent no function on its own, it is a simple element in a product.

Assembly

Involves creating a collection of elements, components, and modules combined into a single unit or entity that performs a single function. Assembly projects may produce a simple stand-alone product (such as a CD player or a coffee machine) or build a subsystem of a larger system (such as automobile transmission).

System

Involves a complex collection of interactive elements and subsystems, jointly performing multiple functions to meet a specific operational need. System projects may build products such as cars, computers, or buildings, or they may deal with the creation of entire new businesses that include several functions.

Array

These projects deal with a large, widely dispersed collection of systems that function together to achieve a common purpose (sometimes they are called "systems of systems" or "super systems"). Examples of arrays include national communication networks, a mass transit infrastructure, or regional power distribution networks, as well as entire corporations.

Figure 15. Diamond approach - Complexity dimension.

The major difference among projects along the complexity

dimension relates to the organizational structure, the formality of

processes, and the way in which project activities are coordinated and

integrated. At the lower end, component and assembly projects are

performed within one organization and very often within one functional

group, with, however, help from other technical functions. At the system

project level, projects typically have a main contractor that is responsible for the delivery of the final product. Array projects are organized differently from projects at the other levels. Managing an array program requires the administration of many separate projects, each devoted to a segment or system. Given the evolutionary development of many arrays, the array project organization typically is established as an ongoing program, to which more segments are continuously added.

Pace

The pace dimension represents the urgency and how much time is available. Pace affects the autonomy of project teams, the bureaucracy, the speed of decision-making, and the intensity of top management involvement. The time available to complete a project has a substantial effect on how a project is managed.

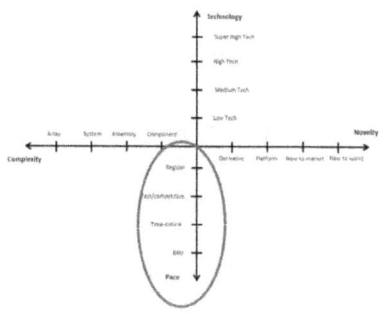

Regular

Regular projects are those efforts where time is not critical to immediate organizational success.

Fast/competitive

These projects are the most common projects carried out by industrial and profit-driven organizations. They are typically conceived to address market opportunities, create a strategic position, or form new business lines.

Time-critical

These projects must be completed by a specific date, which is constrained by a definite event or window of opportunity. Missing the deadline means project failure. Examples might be the launch of a space vehicle based on a specific cosmic constellation, or the Y2K project.

Blitz

Blitz projects are the most urgent, most time-critical. These are crisis projects. Solving the crisis as fast as possible is the criterion for success.

Figure 16. Diamond approach - Pace dimension.

Projects referred to as *regular* pace typically are carried out to achieve long-term or infrastructure goal, but with no real time pressure. Although *regular* pace projects are planned for completion on a certain date, missing the deadline may be tolerated, because time is not critical to immediate organizational success. Whilst, for a *time-critical* project, failing to meet the time goal means project failure. Then, *Blitz* projects fall into a completely different category. They are typically initiated in response to a crisis or as a result of an unexpected event. Examples are wartime events, or the most famous example would be the effort to save the Apollo 13 crew after the craft's fuel tank exploded, when only a few hours were left before oxygen and power would run out (Shenhar & Dvir, 2007, p. 129).

Let us take an example of a real project, which pretty much everyone can relate to – the iPhone 1 and iPhone 6. Not surprisingly, the diamond representing the first iPhone looks a bit different from the iPhone 6. The main difference being that for the first version, the novelty was higher, the technological uncertainty was higher, the complexity was pretty much the same, and the pace was at a lower level than for the later versions. The reason for iPhone 6 being defined as time-critical on the pace dimension, is due to the marketing approach Apple choses for launching new product versions. The date is known to millions of people before market launch.

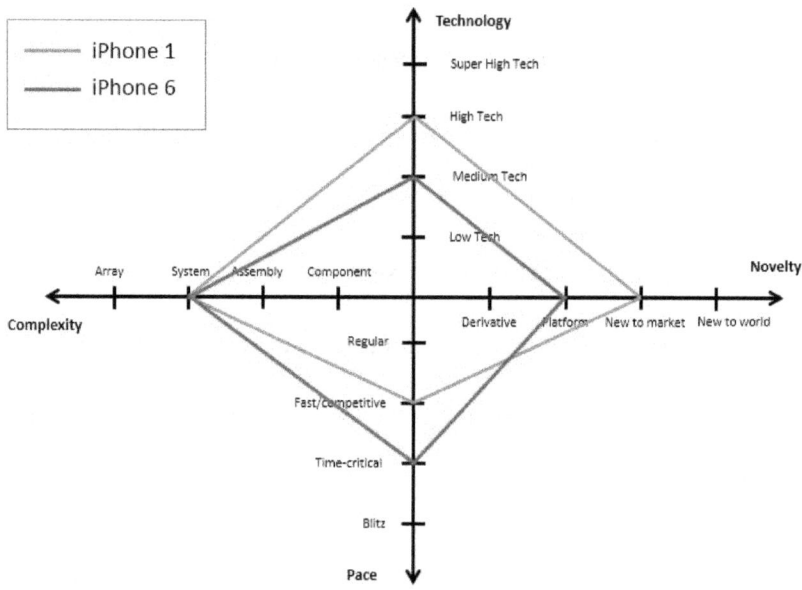

Figure 17. The diamond of iPhone 1 versus iPhone 6.

Let me also give you an example of a diamond for a project I was working on a few years back. The project was called Clean Machine, and this was a very technical OSS transformation project (for those of you familiar with Telecom and Datacom you will nod and think: "yes, complicated stuff").

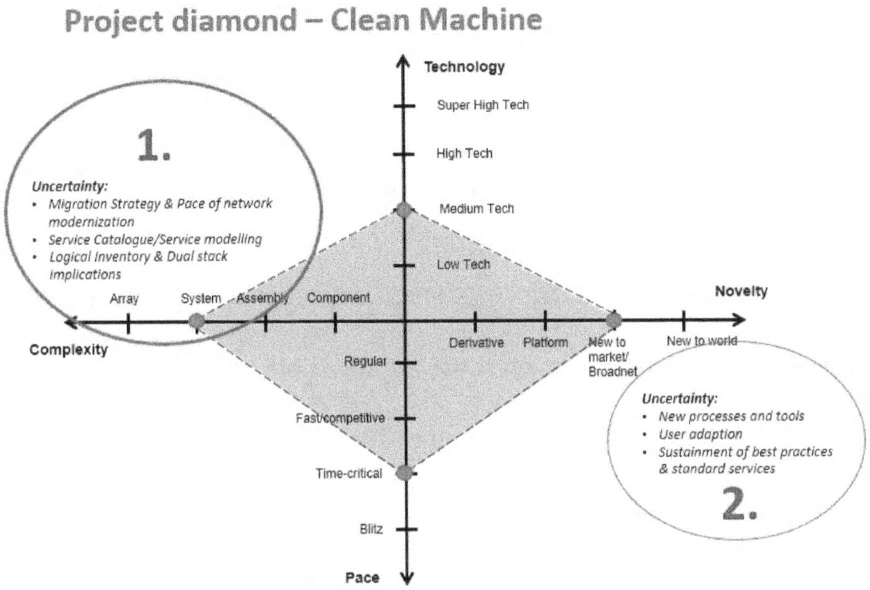

Project diamond – Clean Machine

Figure 18. The diamond for Clean Machine.

I would argue that the ROI for making a diamond for your project would always be way above any other investment option. Seriously, it will take you and your most important stakeholders about 1-2 hours to get a proper view of where the uncertainty lies for your project. It will give you a better assessment of the overall uncertainty, resources needed, contingencies, and selecting the right PM style. It will give you guidance as to how the project should be organized to meet the level of complexity. The rigidness of the project team, the communication language and many other vital discussions can be based on the diamond. *The bigger the diamond, the bigger the challenge, the risk, and the opportunity!*

Failure and success criteria's for projects

According to Shenhar and Dvir (2007) the traditional mind-set maintains that project success depends on satisfying the triple constraint – on time, within budget, and according to specifications. In the dynamic world of business-related projects, however, abiding by the triple constraint is no longer sufficient, and a new model is needed. No matter what the motivation for a project, any assessment of project success must be linked to the parent organization's success and to its well-being in the long run. However, despite numerous arguments, there is still no universal way to measure and assess project success. Meeting time and budget goals is only a small part of the bigger picture. Having achieved such goals suggests that the project was managed carefully and efficiently and that the project team did a good job of planning, monitoring, and executing the plan. But adhering to a project plan tells us nothing about achieving the long-term business goals for which the project was initiated in the first place.

Shenhar and Dvir further argues that project and product success should not be separated. They are two side of the same coin, and both must be addressed by the project team during execution. Based on their own research, they suggest a comprehensive assessment of project success in the short and long term, which can be defined by five basic groups of measures:

1. Project efficiency
2. Impact on customer
3. Impact on team
4. Business and direct success
5. Preparation for the future

The first dimension, *project efficiency*, represent the short-term measure: whether the project has been completed according to plan. We are all familiar with this traditional triple-constraint measure.

The second dimension, *impact on customer*, represents the major stakeholder whose perception is critical to the assessment of project success. This dimension should clearly state how the project's result improved the customer's life or business and how it addressed the customers need. This is in fact the dimension, which includes product performance measures, functional requirements, and technical specifications.

The third dimension, *impact on the team*, reflects how the project affects the team and its members. Good project leaders energize and inspire their team members and make the project a memorable, exciting experience. It measures the extent of team learning and team growth and of team members' newly acquired skills and new professional and managerial capabilities.

The fourth dimension, *business and direct success*, reflects the direct and immediate impact the project has on the parent organization. In the business context, it should assess sales levels, income and profits, as well as cash flow and other financial measures.

The fifth dimension, *preparation for the future*, addresses the long-range benefits of the project. It reflects how well the project helps the organization prepare its infrastructure for the future and how it creates new opportunities.

Project success measure	Key measures
Project efficiency	• Meeting schedule • Meeting budget • Yield • Other efficiencies
Impact on customer	• Meeting requirements and specifications • Benefit to customer • Extent of use • Customer satisfaction and loyalty • Brand name recognition
Impact on team	• Team satisfaction • Team morale • Skill development • Team member growth • Team member retention • No burnout
Business and direct success	• Sales, Profits, Market share • ROI, ROE • Cash flow • Service quality • Cycle time • Organizational measures • Regulatory approval
Preparation for future	• New technology • New market • New product line • New core competency • New organizational capability

Figure 19. Project success measures.

So which of these dimensions are more important? The nature of the dimensions suggest that their relative importance also will shift depending on when you look at them. As pictured in the figure below, we will see that in the short-term, and particularly during project execution, the project efficiency dimension is critical. After the project is complete, however, the importance of this dimension diminishes. As time goes by, it matters less and less whether the project has met its resource constraints, and in most cases, after about a year it is almost irrelevant.

While the second and third dimension – impact on the customer and team – become relevant after project completion, the time to think about them (as well as all the other dimensions) is during the project itself, when you have the power to influence them.

The fourth dimension, business and direct success, becomes significant only later. It usually comes to the foreground after a while, when sales of the project's product start to bring in profit or establish market share. And finally, preparation for the future, which expresses the long-term benefits of the project, affects the organization only after years have passed.

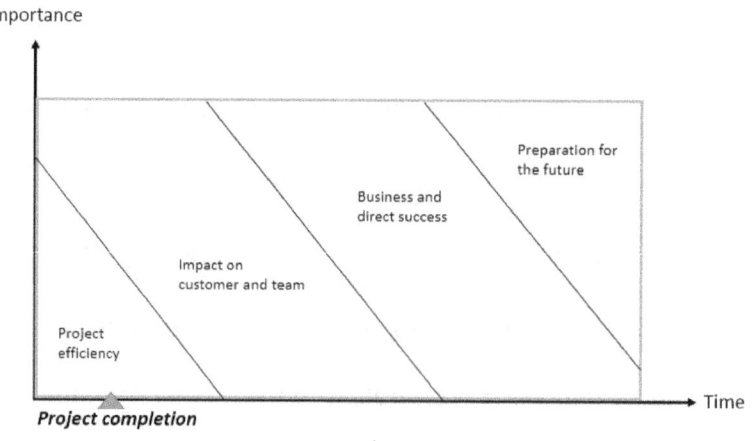

Figure 20. Relative importance of success dimensions.

Similar approaches to measure a projects success has been in use previously. I would like to mention one such method called the *Seven Key's to success* which I have used in previous assignments. This reporting method was developed by IBM around 2002, and the dimensions reported on was carefully chosen from experience in project performance within IBM Business Consulting Services.

Seven dimensions represent the project's success:

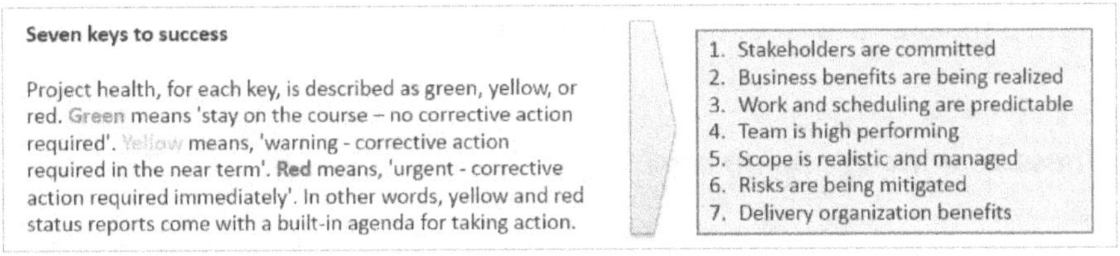

Seven keys to success

Project health, for each key, is described as green, yellow, or red. Green means 'stay on the course – no corrective action required'. Yellow means, 'warning - corrective action required in the near term'. Red means, 'urgent - corrective action required immediately'. In other words, yellow and red status reports come with a built-in agenda for taking action.

1. Stakeholders are committed
2. Business benefits are being realized
3. Work and scheduling are predictable
4. Team is high performing
5. Scope is realistic and managed
6. Risks are being mitigated
7. Delivery organization benefits

Figure 21. Seven Key's to success.

The three dimensions called *Work and scheduling are predictable*, *Team is high performing*, and *Scope is realistic and managed*, represents the direct control and content of any project. On the other hand, the four dimension called *Stakeholders are committed*, *Business benefits are being realized*, *Risks are being mitigated*, and *Delivery organization benefits*, represent the indirect control and the context surrounding the project. Let us just briefly look into each dimension.

Stakeholders are committed

Imagine two very different projects. One includes a CIO who actively works to see the project fail. And he succeeds, and it fails. The other project is for a client who really makes it happen – takes responsibility, makes tough decisions, takes political heat, and truly owns the result.

As a project manager, you will 'fail' in the first project mentioned, and you will have 'success' in the other. As a project manager, we are not the only ones responsible for project outcomes, good or bad.

Business benefits are being realized

Many projects lose their way in terms of business benefits and never get back on track. Too many projects do not have a sound business case in the first place, and should have been saved from a premature death by never having been born. Yes, you can even use this framework to judge the health of projects you are only thinking about doing.

Work and scheduling are predictable

This is the traditional dimension of health. Otherwise known as 'On time and on budget.' Now, anyone can tell you when this one is in serious trouble. In addition, by then, of course, it is often too late to recover. The trickier challenge is to know early in the project if it is likely to do well or not. Here, process and discipline are everything. Why? Because the project team that has the mechanisms for planning and tracking can see the need for a course correction early on. With this type of discipline, there will not be many surprises. (There may be unhappy news, but it will not come as a big surprise to anyone).

Team is high performing

This one is often overlooked, and yet can make a huge difference. It is not just about talent and experience, although these are obviously important. Morale, trust, physical environment, reward and recognition – these are some of the factors that determine sickness or health. It must also be mentioned how powerful it can be to have a truly diverse team – diverse in style, in nationality, in gender, in life experience. It can also be very hard to bring such a team together. Do not let that get to you. Fight for diversity and fight for the time and resources to build trust and communications among your team. I guarantee your project performance will benefit.

Scope is realistic and managed

Get this one right, and 'Work and schedule are predictable' is a lot easier. Get it wrong, and both tend to suffer. My advice is to learn how to be a mean junkyard dog when necessary - and in the nicest possible way, of course.

Risks are being mitigated

Every project has risk. Moreover, the risk picture will change during the project lifetime. The important part of the risk planning in the project is to have mitigation plans, and as soon as we have a plan to reduce or even mitigate the risk totally, the project has done their job. If risks are not properly addressed, and a risk mitigation plan is not developed, the project has not done their job.

Delivery organization benefits

Finally, behind every project, a delivery organization puts it on the line for project management performance. I am not just talking about financial issues. Delivery organizations, whether they are hired consultants or internal IT groups, are trying to enhance reputation, harvest lessons learned, and develop staff with each project. If these aims are kept in sight and continually furthered, the final dimension of project health will be served. If these aims cannot be met, then all parties cannot deem the project a complete success.

Looking back, moving forward

Introduction

"Innovation is about connecting, not inventing (Hargadon, 2003)."

The following topics are covered in this chapter:

- Technology brokering
- The strength of weak ties
- Technology brokering in practice
- The typical technology broker
- 8 rules for innovation through technology brokering

Technology Brokering and Networked Innovation

Process views emphasize that innovation is fundamentally influenced by networks and social interactions including, for example, intra- and inter-firm networks, professional and occupational networks, educational networks, regional networks and so on. Efforts to manage knowledge for innovation must pay attention to the networks (both formal and informal) through which knowledge in specific fields and contexts is produced and communicated, especially where innovation processes span knowledge domains (Newell et al, 2009).

Hargadon has written one of the best books I have read, and it explains the concept of Technology Brokering. This quote from his book is illustrative of his work in the area of breakthrough innovations. *It may take genius to see the potential for breakthrough innovation across a fragmented landscape, but that genius depends more on the network of past wanderings that allows one to see across worlds rather than on any inherent talents* (Hargadon, 2003).

The premise of Hargadon's book, *How Breakthroughs Happen*, is simple. Namely, that breakthrough innovation come by recombining the people, ideas and objects of past technologies. Hargadon (2003) defines technology as the *relationship between people, ideas and objects*. The implication, recalling William Gibson, is that *the future is already here - it is just unevenly distributed.*

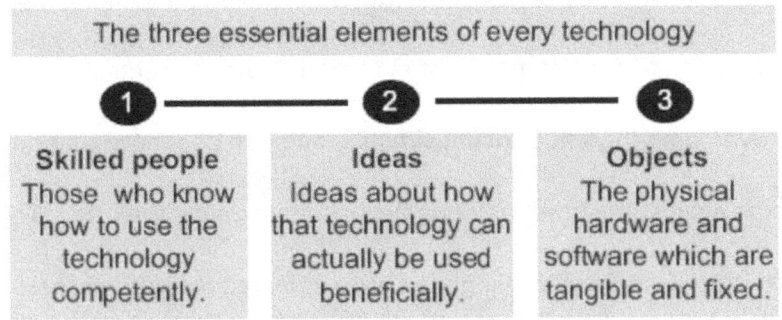

Figure 22. Three essential elements of technology.

Organizations are their own fragmented landscapes, broken into the many small worlds of their divisions, groups, and teams. Organizations are also competitive landscapes. As line managers fight for promotions, for headcount, for budgets, and for their own projects ideas, it is unlikely to look at the organization as a united system, where all employees pull together in the same direction for the common goal of the company. As long as the system is designed this way, who can blame them? More important, who is to say that it is the wrong approach? In fact, according to Andrew Hargadon, this is the right approach. According to him, it is unrealistic to expect that the same people who can compete so ruthlessly in the market will turn around and blithely give it all away to others inside the firm. You cannot turn a large organization into one happy family any more than you can turn a large family into one. He claim that in no organization, no amount of moving speeches, and off-site seminars, is likely to overcome the values of individuality and independence that pit one person against the other and one department against the other. The answer to this, if we listen to Hargadon, is to *embrace the differences*. In the paradox that is innovation, the fragmented groups within large organizations become the source of new ideas in other groups (Hargadon, 2003). From a perspective of recombinant innovation, large firms often have a vast amount of untapped potential.

In fact, companies with internal complexity will find it useful to build *technology brokering groups* building bridges between internal divisions and exploiting what the organization already knows. On the other hand, organizations with few internal divisions and less complexity, will find it more useful to seek outside the organization and link to external technology brokers, rather than establishing internal groups. "Technology brokering" is about *being constantly uncomfortable. It's about never fitting in.*

The strength of weak ties

The theory of the strength of weak ties deserves some explanation. Mark Granovetter, a sociologist at Stanford University, was the first to document the advantages of making connections across a fragmented network. When asked, from a network perspective, how individuals found new jobs, apartments and other valuable resources, most people assume that information flows easily among those people with whom we interact regularly, with whom we share strong ties. Unfortunately, the value of the strong ties tends to be marginal as far as innovation goes; because we know and interact with these people on a regular basis, and we seem to be synchronized on the information we hold. Hence, we are more likely to find valuable and novel information from those whom we have weak ties. Two people share a strong tie when the people they know, know each other; they share a weak tie when the people they know are not connected. According to Granovetter we are more likely to find useful information from those to whom we are weakly tied: casual acquaintances, the friends of brothers, the sisters of neighbours (Hargadon, 2003). A curiosity: In fact, a weak tie made it possible for me to write this book.

Technology Brokering in practice

Many firms can benefit from recognizing that although they might not make good technology brokers, the chances are good that brokers could thrive within their boundaries. There are many places within firms – between project teams, between divisions, between plants – where competition, politics, geography, and lack of communication have created small worlds by creating gaps in the flow of ideas and people across the organization. Here are opportunities for technology brokers to operate within the fragmented landscape of the modern organization, bridging those worlds and building innovative combinations of people, objects, and ideas. Hargadon proposes three different strategies for Technology Brokering: technology brokering as a firm, technology brokering within the firm, and exploiting emergent opportunities for technology brokering.

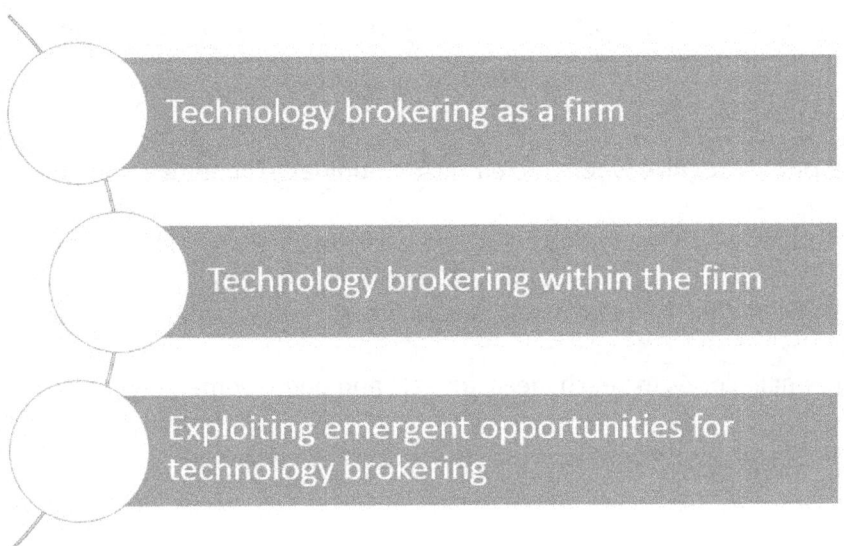

Figure 23. Strategies for Technology Brokering.

The first strategy is the most extreme, and requires that the firm organize itself solely around the process of technology brokering. For these firms, the pursuit of innovation is not a process of deviating from the established routine (or business as usual, if you like), it is business as usual. These firms face the constant pressure to innovate, but they are free to seek out the most effective strategies for gaining access to the technologies of different worlds.

Most firms will not have the possibility to dedicate themselves to the continuous pursuit of innovation. For the rest of us, it is more important to recognize when and where we can create groups within large organizations that can pursue technology brokering strategies full time, or to recognize when to create communities around recombinant innovations when the opportunities emerge. Internal technology brokers will thrive under the same conditions as external ones: where there are many small worlds in which ideas, objects and people emerge and develop, and across worlds, which there is little interaction.

The typical Technology Broker

Moving among different worlds directly shapes people's ability to learn in different contexts and to see how what they have learned might work somewhere else. The advantage, in this case, is to know a little about a lot of things rather than a lot about little. Anybody who acquires deep expertize does so at the expense of breadth. The challenge is to understand how much depth is enough, and how much is too much. The risk is simply in what could have been learned elsewhere but also, how committed individuals and organizations become to their own expertize. Building experiences in many small worlds makes it possible to approach each new problem with a more open mind (Hargadon, 2003, p. 81).

From my own experience, I also find it useful not to be the person with the deepest knowledge about the service or the process in question in my own projects. Why? Because with having the broad knowledge, and not necessarily the deep, I can easily ask questions relevant to the scope, or to the process, which the other team members usually do not ask. In addition, to those of us having experienced group psychology in practice, we know that if the questions are not asked, the group will continue as if everything is ok. I think every project team can benefit from having a person asking, sometimes, the obvious questions, because you will be surprised to find out that there might not be obvious answers to them. In my role as a project manager, or portfolio manager, for that matter, I am conscious about asking these questions – because I know there is value in doing so.

How can we identify a typical technology broker in our organization? Keeping in mind, we are not necessarily talking about "hard" technology here. Remember that we defined technology as the *relationship between people, ideas and objects*. I would argue that more and more technology brokers are entering our organization, whether they themselves are conscious about this or not. During my career, I have seen a few, very distinct technology brokers. Even though, recombinant innovation are relatively rare, and the reason is that the flow of people, ideas and objects among these small worlds are relatively rare. Nevertheless, I would argue that, if you are working in a technical service organization, along with knowledge workers pursuing innovations (incremental or radical), and you do not have any idea who this typical technology broker could be, you and your organization are in trouble.

Based on my own experience, I would say that a typical technology broker often have the following characteristics:

- Curious
- Open-minded
- Social
- Creative
- Experienced
- They often have a large network
- In-depth knowledge of a central product/technological discipline

In short, they have characteristics of both *bridge builders and trenchers*. They have the broad knowledge making them *bridge builders*, and they have in-depth knowledge making them *trenchers*.

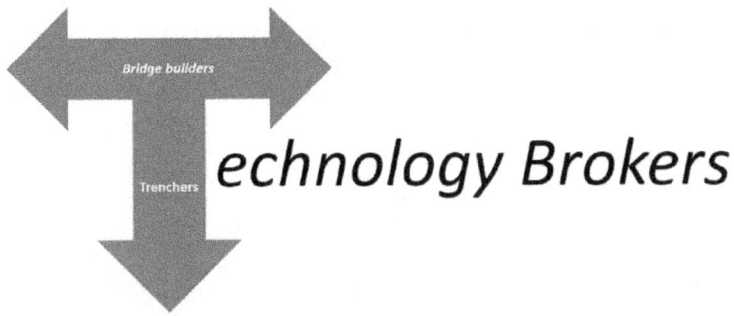

Figure 24. Bridge builders and trenchers – the DNA of a typical Technology Broker.

The fact that they are often curious, social, open-minded and creative makes them the perfect bridge builders. When, in addition, they are equipped with a large network both inside and outside the organization, they have the ability to bridge different worlds. Whether they are conscious about it or not, they are the perfect bridge builders. I have often experienced, that these technology brokers also have a lot of experience (no, they are not rookies) and an in-depth knowledge within a central discipline being concerned with the domain in question, whether it is technical knowledge, process knowledge or any other knowledge. This deep knowledge represent the trenchers in them. People with these characteristics within technical service organization will play an important role in driving innovation. If your organization still have not identified these people, I suggest you make an effort to do so.

8 rules for innovation through technology brokering

Hargadon (2003) concludes with eight rules from his own studies, which emerge as consistent and fundamental to dealing with innovation through *technology brokering*. If you are a technology broker, or you are working with strategies to implement technology brokering within your firm, you should use this as a checklist:

- ***The Future is Already Here***: This attitude simply acknowledges that in moving through distant worlds, other people know something you don't, and you know something they don't. Nothing more and nothing less. The raw materials for the future are already here, they're just unevenly distributed.

- ***Analogy Trumps Invention***: The raw material for breakthrough technologies will come in unexpected forms, the people, the ideas, and the objects will come dressed in other uses, meanings, and other relationships. Untangling these existing resources from their current context and putting them together in new ways require thinking by analogy. It means constantly asking how things are the same. It is all a matter of looking for how things are the same, not for how they are different.

- *Find Your Discomfort Zone:* Technology brokering is about being constantly uncomfortable. It's about never fitting in. The network position that sits across worlds rather within any single one, enabling one to move easily among worlds, is inherently an uncomfortable place to be. Said in another way: if the decisions you make, the budgets you sign, and the projects you initiate are easy – meaning your colleagues would agree with them – then chances are you are thinking within the same boxes they are. If, however, you find that your closest allies reside outside your traditional circles, chances are you're on to something good.

- *Divided We Innovate:* Going back again to the advice from Hargadon, *embrace the differences* rather than tearing down all walls between internal divisions and communities within the organization. It is better to embrace the boundaries in organizations: Those boundaries ensure both the focus needed within each and the variety of best practices that result from that focus. Then find and support the few people who will thrive by moving among these different worlds.

- ***Bridge to Your Strengths:*** Technology brokering isn't about moving into worlds you know little about. It's about finding worlds you know little about but where your own knowledge looks valuable. Bridging to your strengths means moving into those worlds where your past experiences will be valuable contributions, where you are a visitor bearing gifts. Without the ability to contribute in a new place, technology brokers will find it difficult, if not impossible, to work with the best people, the latest thinking, and the critical tools of that world.

- ***Build to Your Weaknesses:*** If two of you agree, then one of you is redundant. This is likely true when it comes to build new ideas, and to recombine people, ideas and objects of past technologies. Think different, together. Forget about the notion of the lone genius. Find one other person who complements your abilities, then another, and then another. The more ties you can build around you, the bigger the collective becomes and the more others become willing to join.

- ***As go the Individuals, So Goes the Organization:*** A common thread appeared in the environments of Hargadon's studies: People embraced technology brokering as a firm (or group, or project) strategy because their own path to success lay in brokering. An individual's value in these organizations came not from any fixed position or authority, but rather from the ability to see connections between what they had seen before and the problems others were facing now. Power, in these firms, did not come from controlling a fixed resource – it came from making new resources out of old experiences.

- **Rip, Mix, Burn:** Describes the ease with which its users can create their own CDs by ripping, mixing and burning a new disc. The tag line may as well be describing the process of innovation. Often, the court must decide which existing people, ideas and objects can be used and which cannot. These decisions determine the direction of innovation in a society because they determine which past ideas, which past objects, and which people can be used again and in which new ways.

I will mention one project that I was managing a few years back. I was working in a debt collection company in Norway, and the task given to us was to automate manual work processes concerned with the debt collection processes. The chief director gave me a very clear mandate – to reduce manual processes by 75%. How we were supposed to accomplish the task, was up to us. Hence, full autonomy was given as to how to execute the project in order to reach the stated goal. As this project was considered a strategic project for the company, I also got to choose my team more or less as I wanted. In other words, a perfect situation for any project manager.

I started out with the obvious people to bring on for this type of project – process specialists, system specialists, architects and test managers. In addition, I got on board a consultant with experience from other industries and other companies – completely outside the debt collection industry. As any team, we had a tough start. In the beginning, it was quite troublesome not having a clear mandate other than the business goal itself. However, as weeks went by we managed to come through the creative process, and think outside the box, and the engagement and "drive" within the project team was something I had never experienced before or after. We designed a concept for automating all debt collection processes into decision trees. This was new to the industry back then, and I have seen many other companies doing the same thing afterwards. The component, which made it possible to make the system for configuring the decision trees, was bought from an independent developer in England.

The project delivered a complete solution that made it possible to reduce the manual work by 65%. We also designed the decision trees so that the ones responsible for the processes within each department could configure changes on their own, not being constantly dependent on IT developers or others to do adjustments along the way.

It is obvious to me, looking back, that the team composition was one major success factor for this project, especially the consultant with a completely different viewpoint than the rest of us (*being the technology broker in this example*). The cooperation within the team was tremendous from a very early stage, and even though I did a few things right as a project manager, I will give most of the credit to the chief director, that understood the importance of total autonomy in this demanding task. This is a good example of technology brokering in practice. This project was not responsible for a radical innovation, but for this company, indeed a huge incremental innovation and, for sure, a process innovation.

Project Entrepreneurs are in fact Technology brokers

I think for many of us, confusion exists as to where project management stops and change management starts, and where change management stops and where technology brokering starts. In addition, to confuse even more, there are other major disciplines present in any change initiative today, spanning areas like innovation, research & development, financial management, resource management, marketing, customer relationship management and more. This means that all project managers today will need to become extremely broad in their profile, and it somehow seems a bit overwhelming.

Aaron Shenhar, in his book Reinventing Project Management (2007), suggests that the diamond approach should be used to help identify potential risks and benefits, and hence, select the right management style. The diamond approach is an analysis tool, which classify a project based on its novelty, technology, complexity, and pace.

First, let us look at some of the specific initiatives that top management can take to implement the ideas of Aaron Shenhar (2007):

- Treat project management as the next core of your competitive assets. Raise the awareness of managers at all levels about the potential of their projects. Make it clear that project management is not the business only for project managers. It should be the business of everyone at every managerial level, as they all have part in project success. Create a career path for project managers, and appoint an executive to become a chief projects officer.

- Treat your projects as investments, not costs. Your investment in projects is perhaps the best investment you can make for your organization, often more important than capital investments.

- Get the best people to lead projects. Avoid the temptation to put your best people in charge of operations. Remember that it is easier to manage operations than complex, uncertain projects. Future operations will be profitable only if the projects that created them were selected correctly, and done well.

- Treat process building as a project. The diamond approach is applicable not only to new product development or construction but also to process building or building process-based services.

- Implement a mechanism to identify failure before it is too late. Use short planning and execution intervals and milestones, and not just dates.

- Implement a policy that encourages project managers to overspend on the up-front planning plus prototyping that will enable quick, small implementations to resolve early unknowns in bigger programs.

Secondly, let us look at how Shenhar exemplifies the difference in management style for different types of projects. In the diamond approach, one of the dimensions to analyse is the *technology* – with levels of uncertainty classified into *Low-tech*, *Medium-tech*, *High-tech* and *Super-high-tech*. Because greater technological uncertainty increases the need to delay the design freeze and conduct more cycles of design, build, and test, it requires a more flexible management style and increased tolerance for ambiguity and uncertainty. In addition, the transition period after design freeze is characterized by an abrupt shift in the project manager's attitude toward change. A high level of flexibility and tolerance for change characterize the project during the initial stage, followed by low or almost no flexibility once the design is frozen. This actually suggest that it might not be the best solution to have the same project manager for one project throughout the entire lifetime.

In low-tech projects, managers must be firm and stick to the initial plan. In medium-tech projects, they should be ready to accept some changes early on, but after design freeze, they should make every effort to get the product out the door as soon as possible.

Highly flexible styles are needed at the higher levels of technological uncertainty. High-tech project managers must be ready to accept many changes and must wait longer for the final product design; and managers of super-high-tech projects must be extremely patient, must live with continuous change, and must make sure that all alternative technologies have been tried. They must also develop an attitude of "look for trouble", since the sooner they can identify problems, the earlier they can fix them.

It is highly likely that a high-tech or super-high-tech project will require a more entrepreneurial leadership style. Why? Because these projects tend to deliver some form of innovation, and we often see radical innovations from such projects. An experienced, business-savvy person best manages the uncertainty within the scope and mandate of such projects. Such projects require far more experience in business development, innovation, technology, market development, and most of all the experience in dealing with uncertainty. I will argue that high-tech and super-high-tech projects will require a person with the unique combination of skills such as project management, change management and technology brokering. In this book, I will refer to such project managers as *project entrepreneurs*. Not only are they familiar with project management with all its constituent skills and knowledge, but they are also technology brokers. They are bridge builders and trenchers. Their abilities are best utilized in the initial stages of complex, and highly technical projects. As the uncertainty has reduced, and the work has reached a far more stable level, the project entrepreneur steps aside, and make place for the more traditional project manager, with an attitude representing far less flexibility towards change.

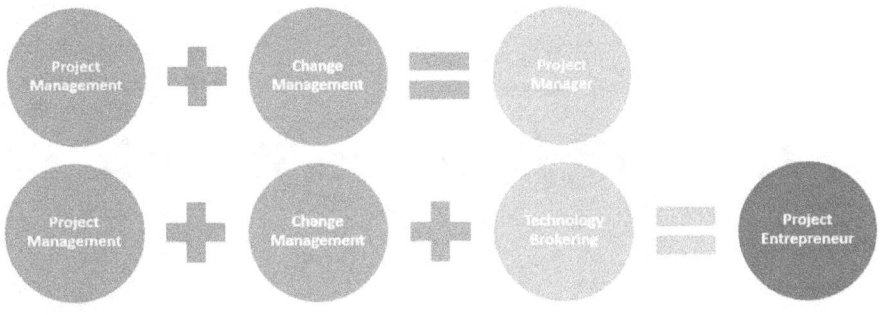

Figure 25. Difference between a Project Entrepreneur and a Project Manager.

I would like to end this chapter by underlining that not everyone has the DNA to become a Project Entrepreneur. Remember: *Technology brokering* is about *being constantly uncomfortable. It's about never fitting in.* My best advice would be for those of you being project managers or project portfolio managers to keep in mind the different managerial styles needed for each change initiative within your organization. We will need both the traditional project manager and the project entrepreneur in all organization. Identifying the project entrepreneurs though, is becoming a critical activity.

Learning from the Starfish

Introduction

"The future is already here, it is just unevenly distributed."

The following topics are covered in this chapter:

- Sweet spot for PPM

- Edge of Chaos

- The value of complexity theory for managers

- The Starfish model

The role of Project Portfolio Management

Project Portfolio Management (PPM) is becoming increasingly popular in the areas of new product development, product and service life cycle management, marketing, engineering, R&D, and the public sector. PPM is applicable in practically any environment where development and delivery of products and services via projects intersect with the use of knowledge workers and technology. Over the same period, the Project Management Institute (PMI) has enjoyed steady growth in membership and is now one of the largest professional associations in the world, boasting more than a 650.000 practitioners in more than 170 countries (pmi.org).

Despite the wide adoption of the PPM practice, together with an increasing body of knowledge in the area of project portfolio management, and a broad range of supporting software applications, many organizations still struggle to fully realize the potential of PPM. Part of this stems from not recognizing and addressing the interconnected nature of portfolio ecosystems and the unique requirements of the modern knowledge worker environment. PMI continuously extend their efforts and best practices into new areas of interest to the whole project management community. Nevertheless, I think it is safe to say that none of us as typical knowledge workers, technology brokers or project entrepreneurs, can rely on finding *one single best way* to handle the complexity and challenges faced by technical service organizations today. We will have to step up and find the right balance ourselves.

In this chapter, I will try my best to form a good starting point for many of us. Forming the detailed recipe for dealing with change in your organization is a demanding task, which ultimately lays with you and your fellow knowledge workers. Looking into the five areas of the Starfish model will trigger you to start thinking of change in a broader perspective, and you will be better equipped to dress up the management team within your organization.

This chapter summarizes the main topics discussed previously; knowledge work and innovation, systems thinking, strategic project leadership, technology brokering and project portfolio management.

Sweet spot for PPM

While focusing on a collection of formal projects is certainly a valid use of the portfolio management discipline, employing such an approach fails to deliver on the promise of PPM. The reason for this is that the availability

of resources for project work is often directly and substantially affected

by other concurrent *run-the-business* activities. In such a scenario, it is

important that you approach project management as a subset of the

overall portfolio of work. How the various elements of project planning

and execution intersect with other areas of work and resource

management presents the central challenge to managing the modern

business environment. Durbin and Doerscher (Taming Change, 2010)

found that supplementing common PPM methods with these practices

ensure successful execution of the complete portfolio of work and

increases the overall effectiveness of the organization and its resources.

Some of the key elements are listed here:

1. **Being flexible**: Martial arts teach us that it is often better to

    leverage the opposing force's momentum than to bluntly resist it.

    Similarly, the realities of today's fast-moving business

    environment must be embraced rather than opposed; no amount

    of denial will overcome the internal and external influences that

    force change on a TSO environment.

2. **Taking a resource-centric approach**: Manage the workload of

    those people with critical skills (typically knowledge workers) by factoring in all of the demand, instead of just the needs of a few major projects. Planning work to avoid reactive juggling of staff and to limit inefficient starts and stops is the key to moving from chaos to success. The result is greater control over assigned work and higher morale for workers who are able to maintain greater focus, be more efficient, and meet realistic expectations.

3. **Operating within the limits of the planning horizon**: The considerations of the planning horizon are equally important when it comes to planning the details of work and resources. That is, how far forward and to what degree you are able to make a reliable plan. If you attempt to plan at a great level of detail too far in advance, emerging changes in work priorities or availability will likely cause staff re-assignments.

4. **Recognizing that work and resource management are inseparable functions**: During planning and execution, recognize the interrelationships between managing work and managing resources. Each is wholly dependent on the other to develop viable plans and successfully accomplish work. The level of detail that you can apply to resource planning and assignment is predicated on the level of detail you have about the work to be

accomplished and vice versa. Due to short time resource

bottlenecks, it could be a good idea to set the priorities by looking

at available resources, rather than the other way around. Realism

in planning is king.

Edge of Chaos

The *edge of chaos* phenomenon was discovered independently by the

physicist and mathematician Norman Packard, a member of the

Dynamical Systems Collective, and Chris Langton, working on the

information systems at the University of Arizona (Gleick, 1987). The edge

of chaos is the *narrow transition zone between order and chaos that is*

extremely conducive to the emergence of novel patterns of behaviours. A

system driven to the edge of chaos is likely to exhibit the sort of

spontaneous processes of self-organization. The edge of chaos notion has

been proven powerful in many different fields, including management

and organizations (Michael C. Jackson, 2003).

Why is this phenomenon interesting in the context of innovation

and change? Because it might be useful to take learnings from the

discipline of systems thinking, chaos and complexity theory, and exploit

whether these learnings somehow can we transferred into another context: namely our fast-moving business environments. Please, be patient, you might actually see the relevance here.

Stacey (1996) use the edge of chaos concept to articulate the most detailed account of how learning and self-organization can be promoted in organizations. He notes the complexity theory conclusion that all complex adaptive systems can operate in one of three zones: a stable zone, an unstable zone and at the edge of chaos, *a narrow transition between stability and instability*. In the stable zone they ossify, in the unstable zone they disintegrate, but at the edge of chaos spontaneous processes of self-organization occur and innovative patterns of behaviours can emerge. This, therefore, seems to be the best place for organizations to be. At the edge of chaos, in a state of *boundary instability,* they behave like dissipative structures and display their full potential for creativity and innovation.

The edge of chaos is difficult to reach and sustain because it requires a kind of balance between the forces promoting stability in an organization and those continuously challenging the status quo. In Stacey's terms, it demands an appropriate degree on tension between an organization's *'legitimate system'* and its *'shadow system'* (or between safety and chaos). The legitimate system consists of the dominant corporate culture and those structures, processes and power hierarchies that support it. It promotes 'ordinary management' in pursuit of the organizations objectives and is essential for ensuring the efficient delivery of products and services, and for containing conflict and anxiety. If it becomes too dominant, however, because the shadow system is not functioning properly, it can constrain all opposition, prevent questioning of objectives, kill double-loop learning and stop all change. The shadow system of an organization consists of those informal aspects that harbour the potential for contradiction, conflict and change. It works well when it generates new ways of thinking that challenge the legitimate system and threatens, by bringing forth sufficient tension and crisis, to replace at least some parts of that system. If the shadow system becomes too dominant, however, because the legitimate system is unable to check the positive feedback loops produced by instability, anarchy can result. The shadow system sabotages pursuit of objectives, levels of anxiety rise among the workforce preventing creativity and double-loop learning, and the system enters the unstable zone and disintegrates.

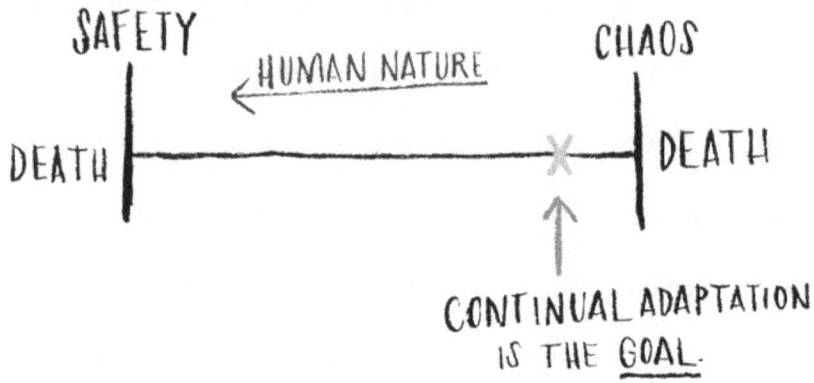

Figure 26. Edge of chaos.

The edge of chaos, the preferable state, demands therefore that creative tension be maintained between the legitimate and shadow systems (noted as safety and chaos in the figure above). The legitimate system must provide clear guidelines, authorize appropriate structures and procedures, and contain anxiety among the personnel. At the same time, the shadow system must give rise to a diversity of perspectives. The shadow system is the source of innovation, contention and political struggle as different groups engage in dialogue and learning, end entertain alternative to the status quo (Michael C. Jackson, 2003, p. 123).

As continual adaption is the goal for any organization (at least the ones that are keen on long term survival), this powerful phenomenon is something to be aware of. Further, by understanding the forces between the legitimate system and the shadow system, and being aware of which co-worker is leaning towards stability and which is leaning towards chaos, you could actually make intentional decisions creating more tension between the two forces, hence moving you towards the edge of chaos.

The value of complexity theory to managers

Traditional management theory advises managers what to do in order to achieve goals in an optimum way. It teaches them how to organize the parts of an enterprise into a coherent structure. It seeks conformity from employees and puts in place detailed control procedures to ensure that this is being realized. Michael C. Jackson, in his book Systems Thinking, refers to the work of Peter Fryer (www.trojanmice.com) and his five lessons that managers can easily learn from complexity theory:

1. The most important thing that managers can do is *change their way of thinking*, abandoning mechanism and determinism, and learning to appreciate and cope with their relationships, dynamism and unpredictability.

2. Organization *coevolve with their environments* (remember the Viable Systems Model?), and therefore managing relationships

with the environment is crucial. This means being prepared to respond to the environment, adapting as necessary but also being ready to grasp opportunities as they present themselves.

3. The best managers are able to *intuitively grasp the patterns that are driving the behaviour of their organizations* and the environments they are confronting. The look for patterns in the whole and seek small changes that can have the maximum impact on unfavourable patterns.

4. The most successful organization *do not try to control everything*. To an extent managers can trust in chaos and allow the processes operating at the edge of chaos to bring new order through self-organization.

5. So that organizations have the best chance of understanding those patterns that do exist and responding to the unpredictable, managers should encourage learning, diversity and a variety of opinion.

Finding the right balance for dealing with change

Today's workforce is far less homogenous than in the past. In other words, today's professional knowledge workers are individuals in every respect. They are also more educated, culturally diverse, motivated and mobile. There is a mutual expectation that knowledge worker professionals will be largely self-directed.

It is already challenging to deal with change. When that change primarily relies on knowledge workers, the situation has become even more challenging. Knowledge work is difficult to plan, estimate, supervise and oversee. This brings new challenges into the project-way-of-working. Sticking to traditional project methodologies will simply not be sufficient for any organization. For the majority of change initiatives within your organization you will need to include several other ingredients to succeed, be optimally equipped, and find the right balance.

The Starfish model

From Wikipedia:

Starfish or sea stars are star-shaped echinoderms belonging to the class Asteroidea. About 1,500 species of starfish occur on the seabed in all the world's oceans, from the tropics to frigid polar waters. They are found from the intertidal zone down to abyssal depths, 6,000 m (20,000 ft) below the surface. Starfish have tube feet operated by a hydraulic system and a mouth at the centre of the oral or lower surface. They are opportunistic feeders and are mostly predators on benthic invertebrates. Several species have specialized feeding behaviours including eversion of their stomachs and suspension feeding. They have complex life cycles and can reproduce both sexually and asexually. Most can regenerate damaged parts or lost arms and they can shed arms as a means of defence. Starfish are keystone species in their respective marine communities. Their relatively large sizes, diverse diets and ability to adapt to different environments makes them ecologically important.

A keystone species is a species that has a disproportionately large effect on its environment *relative to its abundance*. Such species are described as playing a critical role in maintaining the structure of an ecological community, affecting many other organisms in an ecosystem and helping to determine the types and numbers of various other species in the community. Without keystone species, the ecosystem would be dramatically different or cease to exist altogether.

What I suggest is that you widen your horizon and take into consideration some of the theory presented in this book, and by that, become better equipped to deal with change in your organization.

The Starfish model sums up the essence of this book. In the same way that the Starfish represent a keystone species that plays a unique and crucial role in the way an ecosystem functions, the Starfish model will play a unique and crucial role in the way your organization can deal with change. The project triangle, the traditional management models for dealing with change, is simply not sufficient to make sure that your business will survive in an ever-changing environment. Summarized below is the key take-away from the five elements of the Starfish model.

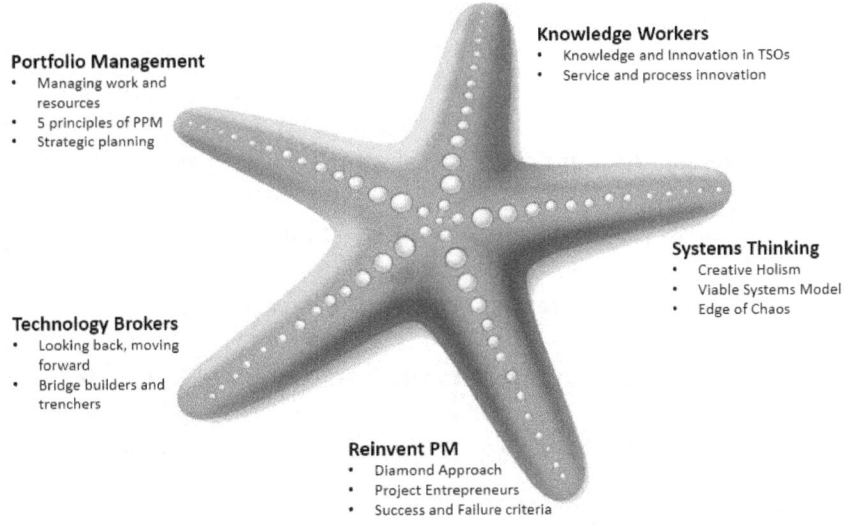

Knowledge Workers
- Knowledge and Innovation in TSOs
- Service and process innovation

Portfolio Management
- Managing work and resources
- 5 principles of PPM
- Strategic planning

Systems Thinking
- Creative Holism
- Viable Systems Model
- Edge of Chaos

Technology Brokers
- Looking back, moving forward
- Bridge builders and trenchers

Reinvent PM
- Diamond Approach
- Project Entrepreneurs
- Success and Failure criteria

Figure 27. The Starfish model.

Managing Knowledge Workers and Innovation

I started this book by presenting an organization's main activities: *business as usual* and *change*. This is nothing but a hunch, but I feel convinced that most organizations do not realize what portion of total efforts within the organization is spent on change (or should have been spent on change). In my opinion, most organizations still have a way to go before the can fully utilize the momentum of knowledge workers in reaching their strategic goals.

Knowledge workers reside in an opportunity-rich environment – they simultaneously facilitate change and manage ongoing operations (business as usual). As mentioned earlier, managing knowledge work and knowledge workers is arguably the single most important challenge being faced by all kinds of organizations. This is because innovation is so central to knowledge work, and knowledge work is so central to innovation. Many of the unique skills and experiences of knowledge workers would be largely wasted if they were not provided with the right opportunities to innovate. Innovation is becoming more and more an art in managing knowledge workers (due to the service economy). Hence, knowledge is becoming the main source of competitive advantage.

Having Google practices in mind it is obvious that management need to put employee morale and satisfaction high up on the strategic agenda in order to earn the needed loyalty and engagement from their knowledge workers. Knowledge workers will need more autonomy then before, they will demand more flexibility than before, and they will need to interact with more people than before. Using traditional models for management on knowledge workers will not be sufficient to deal with today's pace of change and innovation.

One last thing to mention regarding knowledge work – is the *"epistemology of possession"* and *"epistemology of practice"*. Managers need to consider the best way to organize the environment for knowledge workers so that they easily can connect with each other. Striving to increase the knowledge level for each knowledge worker might not be the answer, but connecting the widely distributed knowledge from a *epistemology of practice* point of view should be considered carefully in understanding how knowledge can be managed to achieve innovation.

Systems Thinking and complexity

Simplicity is rarely effective in the face of complexity, change and diversity.

From systems thinking theory we have learned that a more holistic view is needed to see the structures that underlie complex situations, and for discerning high from low leverage change. Fundamentally, simple solutions fail because they are not holistic or creative enough. Sub optimization is a result of not being holistic enough, and by concentrating on the parts of the system, rather than the whole.

Stafford Beer re-defined the term cybernetics into organizational cybernetics by calling it *the science of effective organizations*. He was determined to break with the traditional management thinking. He came up with the *Viable Systems Model* (VSM). By transferring the study of the human being into the organizational context, he made it possible to increase the understanding of the behaviour of complex organizations. In essence, the viable systems model is about the design of organizations as adaptive, goal-seeking entities.

The holistic view from systems thinking can easily be linked to the theory of technology brokering. I will connect the dots here by referring to the term *creative holism*. Creative holism makes you able to recognise the limitations of a given perspective, and to see how situations and problems can be framed, and reframed in different ways. This will allow new solutions to emerge. The people best skilled for creative holism, are Technology Brokers.

The *edge of chaos* is an extremely powerful phenomenon to be aware of. The edge of chaos is described *as the narrow transition zone between order and chaos that is extremely conducive to the emergence of novel patterns of behaviours*. A system driven to the edge of chaos is likely to exhibit some sort of spontaneous processes of self-organization. The challenge, though, is to sustain the balance between the forces promoting stability (the legitimate system) and the forces continuously challenging the status quo (the shadow system). An organization that is not aware of this phenomenon will not only be unable to exploit the emergence of novel patterns of behaviours, but will also risk that either the legitimate system or the shadow system is too dominant.

Project Entrepreneurship and choosing the right management style

Every project is unique, but they also have a lot in common. The question becomes how to identify the commonalities and differences and allow managers to classify their projects and choose the right approach for each project. Shenhar & Dvir (2007) recommend the *Diamond approach* as a framework in which the project management style can be tailored to the circumstances, environment, and task. The traditional model, being basically, the *triple constraint* and the *one size fits all approach*, is only viable for a small group of projects today.

The major challenge faced by all organizations is to deal properly with uncertainty in projects. With the diamond approach, organizations are equipped with a model to adapt to the dynamics of the environment, technology and markets. For example, higher technological uncertainty increases the need to delay the design freeze and conduct more cycles of design, build, and test. Hence, it requires a more flexible management style and increased tolerance for ambiguity and uncertainty. At a later stage (typically after design freeze) the tolerance and flexibility decreases drastically, and planning and preparing for a shift in project management style does not sound like a bad idea at all.

Project entrepreneurs are needed in high-tech and super-high-tech projects to deal with complexity, continuous change, and high degree of uncertainty for long periods of time. The project entrepreneur will take on more responsibilities than the ordinary project manager. The project entrepreneur will be responsible for both project success and product success. They are in fact dealing with innovation – in one way or the other.

The last essential take-away from Shenhar & Dvir's book on re-inventing project management is the *assessment of project success* in the short and long term. Again, they argue that project and product success should not be separated. They are two sides of the same coin, and both must be addressed by the project team during execution. They suggest five measures of project success in the short and long term:

- Project efficiency
- Impact on the customer
- Impact on the team
- Business and direct success
- Preparation for the future

While the first measure is a short-term measure (and the traditional triple constraint measure), the other four measures are of a more long-term nature. As times goes by it matters less and less whether the project has met its short-term efficiency measures, and in most cases, after a year or so it is almost irrelevant. While the traditional project manager typically will focus on the short-term measures like project efficiency, the project entrepreneur (when given the needed autonomy) will likely focus more on the long-term measures like impact on the customer/team, business and direct success, and preparation for the future.

Technology Brokers – the future is already here

Innovation is about connecting, not inventing.

Hargadon (2003) defines technology as *the relationship between people, ideas and objects*. He argues that breakthrough innovation come by recombining the people, ideas and objects of past technologies. Hence, *the future is already here, it is just unevenly distributed.* Networks and social interactions fundamentally influence innovation, which is why organization will need to pay attention to the formal and informal networks through which knowledge is produced and communicated.

The typical *technology broker* often have the following characteristics: curious, open-minded (they often utilize and interact with weak ties), social, creative, experienced (in-depth knowledge of one or several disciplines), and equipped with a large network. In short, they have the characteristics of both *bridge builders and trenchers*. They have the broad knowledge making them bridge builders, and they have in-depth knowledge making them trenchers. Project entrepreneurs are indeed *technology brokers*. Not all technology brokers are project

entrepreneurs though. Being a project entrepreneur requires not only the

DNA of a technology broker, but also the skills and experiences required

for project and change management.

Hargadon has an interesting viewpoint on the organization and

the fragmented landscapes within them. Controversially, but nevertheless

logically, he argues that the competitive "silos" within an organization

should be embraced rather than united. In the paradox that is innovation,

the fragmented groups within large organizations become the source of

new ideas in other groups. Technology brokering groups are enabled to

build bridges between internal divisions and exploiting what the

organization already knows. This is the most common technology

brokering strategy: *technology brokering within the firm*.

Last, but not least, since technology brokers are not in abundance,

and the innovative capacity of your organization is dependent on

recombining the people, ideas and objects of past technologies, I suggest

you start identifying the technology brokers within your organization. If

you are lucky enough to be equipped with technology brokers that also

have the skills and experiences from project and change management,

you might be on to something good.

Portfolio Management – dealing with change capacity

Portfolio management is a set of disciplined processes for making smart business decisions on change events. The most important questions asked in the context of portfolio management are: Does your portfolio represent the *optimum allocation of resources* in context of the organization's strategic objectives, available resources and risk or achievability? Is the portfolio *sufficient* and *necessary*?

The fundamental advantage of portfolio management lies in how it enables you to address the demands placed on the organization so that you can produce the greatest value with the capacities that you have available. What capacities are we talking about here? Correct. Both *money* AND *people*. Remember, you can put excess money in the safe or the savings account, but the effort of your people cannot be stored or put on hold. Like water over the dam, *every hour of effort passed is in constant flow*. This is especially the case for knowledge intensive industries. Taking a resource-centric approach becomes crucial in dealing with resource and capacity management for any organization.

Next to the resource and capacity management process, you should have a proper project prioritization process in place. If this process is not in place, the portfolio management process will suffer. Why? Because you cannot truly be sure that your portfolio represent the *optimum allocation of resources* in context of the organization's strategic objectives, available resources and risk or achievability, unless you have a clear sight of the priorities within your portfolio, and their link to the strategic objectives.

Strategic planning is therefore at the very core of portfolio management. Strategic planning sets the context within which portfolio management operates by providing the basis for determining the scope of the portfolio and the prioritization of individual initiatives (projects). Certain principles holds true for any organization to be able to succeed with portfolio management, and meeting the organization's strategic agenda:

- Senior management commitment
- Governance alignment
- Strategy alignment
- Portfolio office
- Energized change culture

Afterword

Author's Background

I have an educational background from a four-year programme in economics and business administration consisting of three years at bachelor/undergraduate level and one year at master/graduate level. In addition, I have taken two additional master programs at the Norwegian School of Business within the fields of Innovation and Leadership. I am a certified practitioner from the Project Management Institute, holding the title of PMP (Project Manager Professional), and PMI-ACP (Agile Certified Practitioner), and I hold the titles MSP (Managing Successful Programs), SPL (Strategic Project Leader), and MoP (Foundation Certificate in Portfolio Management).

Permission to Use

Feel free to use the material in any way you see fit, as long as you identify the source.

Acknowledgments

Because of the casual manner in which this book was prepared, many citations of authors were unfortunately not included. I apologize for not being more diligent in identifying the specific passages.

- *How Breakthroughs Happen*, Andrew Hargadon, Harvard Business School Press, Boston, 2003.
- *Systems thinking, Creative Holism for Managers*, Michael C. Jackson, John Wiley & Sons, West Sussex, 2003.
- *Taming Change with Portfolio Management,* Pat Durbin, Terry Doerscher, Greenleaf Book Group Press, Austin, 2010.
- *Reinventing Project Management*, Arron J. Shenhar, Dov Dvir, Harvard Business Review Press, Boston, 2007.
- *Managing Knowledge Work and Innovation,* Newell, Robertson, Scarbrough, Swan, Palgrave Macmillan, Hampshire, 2009.

- *Organisasjon og ledelse,* Lee G. Bolman, Terrence E. Deal, Gyldendahl Norsk Forlag, Oslo, 2012.

- *Competing in a Service Economy*, Anders Gustafsson, Michael D. Johnson, John Wiley & Sons, San Francisco, 2003.

- *The Innovators Solution,* Clayton M. Christensen, Michael E. Raynor, Harvard Business School Press, Boston, 2003.

- *Mastering the Dynamics of Innovation,* James M. Utterback, Harvard Business School Press, Boston, 1996.

Glossary

Introduction

This chapter serves as a reference for relevant terms connected to the theory used within the book; covering innovation, knowledge work, systems thinking, change management, project management, and portfolio management.

Definitions

Term	Definition
Base services	Base services represent the continuum of level-of-effort work needed to deliver existing products and services at current production and quality levels, and to generally maintain the supporting assets and operations of your organization.
Baseline	An approved plan for a project, plus or minus approved changes.
BAU	The way the business normally achieves its objectives.

Brown Cow	The purpose of the Brown Cow analysis is to get a common understanding of the problem at hand (headache), and a good description of the goal and the organizational need (target) without thinking about the solution. The method will help you assure that you are finding a good solution to the right problem.
Change control	Identifying, documenting, approving or rejecting, and controlling changes to the project baseline.
Change management	Change management refers to any approach to transitioning individuals, teams, and organizations using methods intended to re-direct the use of resources, business process, budget allocations, or other modes of operation that significantly reshape a company or organization. CM focuses on how people and teams are affected by an organizational transition.
Cybernetics	The science of control and communication in the animal and the machine. Redefined by Beer: Science of effective organization.
Diamond approach	The diamond approach offers a disciplined tool for assessing a project's benefits and risks and for selecting the right project management style. It also gives you a model for assessing a project at midcourse, and for putting a troubled project back on track. The diamond model includes four dimensions to distinguis among projects: novelty, technology, complexity, and pace.
Dominant design	A dominant design in a product is, by definition, the one that wins the allegiance of the marketplace, the one that competitors and innovators must adhere to if they hope to command significant market following.

Earned Value (EV)	The value of work performed expressed in terms of the approved budget assigned to that work for a schedule activity or work breakdown structure component. Also referred to as the budgeted cost of work performed.
Earned Value Management (EVM)	A management methodology for integrating scope, schedule, and resources, and for objectively measuring project performance and progress.
Edge of chaos	Edge of chaos is the narrow transition zone between order and chaos that is extremely conducive to the emergence of novel patterns of behaviours.
Entrepreneurship	The pursuit of opportunity beyond the resources you currently control.
Governance	Establishment of policies, and continuous monitoring of their proper implementation, by the members of the governing body of an organization. It includes the mechanisms required to balance the powers of the members (with the associated accountability), and their primary duty of enhancing the prosperity and viability of the organization.
Hard systems thinking	Methodologies such as Operational Research (OR), Systems Analysis (SA), and Systems Engineering (SE), focusing on objective and mathematical models.
Holism	Holism is an alternative to reductionism. Holism is looking at the system as more than the sum of its parts, as the whole system is affected by the relationships between the parts of the system.
Incremental innovation	A series of small improvements to existing product, service, process, organization or method

	whose performance has been significantly enhanced or upgraded.
Industry Work	Industry work is routine-work. The basis of the operation is the structure of activities.
Innovation	Production or adoption, assimilation, and exploitation of a value-added novelty in economic and social spheres; renewal and enlargement of products, services, and markets; development of new methods of production; and establishment of new management systems. It is both a process and an outcome.
Knowledge	The ability to discriminate within and across contexts.
Knowledge Work	Knowledge work is non-routine work. The basis of the operation is the knowledge of individuals.
Organizational knowledge	A learned set of norms, shared understanding and practices that integrates actors and artefacts to produce value outcomes within a specific social and organizational context.
Other planned work	Other planned work constitutes the organizational demands that fall in between base services and strategic initiatives. This includes shorter-term activities that are beyond level-of-effort operations such as noncapital maintenance and enhancement projects; emerging major break-fix activities, and making incremental, evolutionary improvements.
Portfolio	An organization's portfolio is the totality of its investment (or segment thereof) in the changes required to achieve its strategic objectives.
Portfolio Governance	Encompasses the structures, accountabilities and policies, standards and process for decision-

	making within an organization in order to answer the key strategic questions "Are we doing the right things?", "Are we doing them the right way?" and "Are we realizing the benefits?".
Portfolio Management	Portfolio management is a coordinated collection of strategic processes and decisions that together enable the most effective balance of organizational change and BAU (business as usual).
Program	A program is a temporary, flexible organization created to coordinate, direct and oversee the implementation of a set of related projects and activities in order to deliver outcomes and benefits related to the organization's strategic objectives.
Program Management	The centralized coordinated management of a program to achieve the program's strategic objectives and benefits.
Project	A project is a temporary endeavour undertaken to create a unique product, service or result.
Project Entrepreneur	The project entrepreneur will take on more responsibilities than the ordinary project manager. The project entrepreneur will be responsible for both project success and product success.
Project Management	The application of knowledge, skills, tools, and techniques to project activities to meet the project requirements.
Project Manager (PM)	The person assigned by the performing organization to achieve the project objectives.
P3M3	The portfolio, programme and project management maturity model, which provides a

	framework with which organizations can assess their current performance and put in place improvement plans.
Radical innovation	A radical or disruptive innovation is one that has a significant impact on a market and on the economic activity of firms in that market.
Reductionism	*Reductionism* sees the parts as paramount and seeks to identify the parts, understand the parts and work up from an understanding of the parts to an understanding of the whole.
Soft systems thinking	Soft systems thinking abandon the notion that it is possible to assume easily identifiable, agreed-on goals, that can be used to provide an objective account of the system and its purpose. Soft systems thinking make subjectivity central, working with a variety of world views during the methodological process.
Sponsor	The person or group that provides the financial resources, in cash or in kind, for the project.
Stakeholder	Person or organization (e.g., customer, sponsor, performing organization, or the public) that is actively involved in the project, whose interests may be positively or negatively affected by execution or completion of the project. A stakeholder may also exert influence over the project and its deliverables.
Strategy	The approach or line to take, designed to achieve a long-term aid. Strategies can exist at different levels in an organization.
Strategic initiatives	Strategic initiatives are major changes of operational significance. Typically, this class of demand constitutes the portfolio of formally managed projects, including new product

	development.
Strategic planning	Strategic planning is an organization's process of defining its strategy, or direction, and making decisions on allocating its resources to pursue this strategy.
System	A system is a complex whole, the functioning of which depends on its parts and the interactions between those parts. Examples of systems are river systems, living organisms, automobiles, families and human activity.
Systems thinking	Systems thinking is a discipline for seeing the "structures" that underlie complex situations, and for discerning high from low leverage change. Ultimately, it simplifies life by helping us to see the deeper pattern lying beneath the events and the details.
Viable System Model (VSM)	The viable system model represents a design of organizations as adaptive, goal-seeking entities. The model assumes that the environment surrounding the organization is of much greater variety than the organizations itself, and that the organization is in turn of a much greater variety than the management
Technology	The relationship between people, ideas and objects.
Technology Broker	A technology broker often have the following characteristics: curious, open-minded (they often utilize and interact with weak ties), social, creative, experienced, and equipped with a large network. In short, they have the characteristics of both bridge builders and trenchers. They have the broad knowledge making them bridge builders, and they have in-depth knowledge making them

	trenchers.
Technology Brokering	The idea of technology brokering is to span multiple, otherwise disconnected industries, to see how existing technologies could be used to create breakthrough innovations in other markets.
Technical Service Organizations (TSOs)	Technical service organization rely on knowledge workers. The typical competence held by knowledge workers span over areas such as engineering services, product development, research and development, and IT services.

www.ingramcontent.com/pod-product-compliance
Lightning Source LLC
Chambersburg PA
CBHW051208170526
45165CB00013B/548